"Awfully good. In the often brutally candid (and therefore redemptive) witness of Kurt Armstrong, there are no corners of human experience beyond the interest and affection of God's inescapably earthbound economy. With wit, verve, and eye-rubbingly honest straightforwardness, Armstrong presents the self (his self and ours) as the inescapably social gift of others and life in God as the identity we hold to loosely to find, again and again, in the sacred everyday. With one feat of attentiveness after another, he expands the space of the talkaboutable."

—David Dark
author of *The Sacredness of Questioning Everything*

"Armstrong's reflections on love and marriage are romantic and cynical, restless and content, sentimental and pragmatic. His recollections are an exercise in making sense of it all. Marriage is life. He wants to pass on to us, not self-help or relationship techniques, but a habit of thinking. Marriage offers the depth of life, both sin and grace, and to examine it more deeply is to live it more fully."

—David M. McCarthy
author of *Sex and Love in the Home*

"In the tradition of writers like Wendell Berry and Kathleen Norris, Kurt Armstrong here presents a gathering of carefully crafted essays which take life, marriage, parenthood, and language itself, with deep seriousness. While this young writer challenges consumerist assumptions with conviction, his voice never becomes pedantic. Coupled with deep conviction and sincerity is a kind of vulnerability and transparency that keeps his own humanity fully in view. In a day of flippant wisecracking about even sacred subjects, Kurt Armstrong's lucid and honest pieces come like a cool stream, refreshing our spirits while renewing our vision. We will look for much more from this young writer."

—Maxine Hancock
editor of *Christian Perspectives on Gender, Sexuality, and Community*

"Somehow, after reading *Why Love Will Always Be a Poor Investment*, marriage as we know it in North America is no longer possible, and that's a good thing. With wit, imagination, satire, and a brilliant awareness of the cultural hurdles we face, Armstrong clarifies what a new faithfulness might mean for those of us seeking to be married in these times. Thank you Kurt Armstrong for this book!"

—David Fitch
author of *The Great Giveaway*

"Kurt Armstrong makes an eloquent case for marriage as a life-long commitment and radical act against the background of our consumer culture. His arguments are fleshed out, lovingly, in the story of his own marriage, the place where he has found his home. It's a book that will inspire and encourage readers in their own journeys."

—Sharon Gallagher
editor of *Radix* magazine

Why Love

Will Always Be

A Poor Investment

Why Love
Will Always Be
A Poor Investment

Marriage and Consumer Culture

KURT ARMSTRONG

WIPF & STOCK · Eugene, Oregon

WHY LOVE WILL ALWAYS BE A POOR INVESTMENT
Marriage and Consumer Culture

A version of "Locust Years" was broadcast on *The Vinyl Café* on CBC Radio 2.

"Jesus Loves Your Penis, Son" was originally published in *Geez* magazine.

A version of "Let All Striving Cease" was originally published in *Radix* magazine and is reprinted with permission.

"Why Love Will Always Be A Poor investment" is reprinted with permission from: *Where Faith Meets Culture: The Radix Magazine Anthology* (Wipf and Stock.)

"Loves," Copyright © 2002 by Scott Cairns, from *Philokalia* (Zoo Press). Used by permission.

"Marriage" and "Goods," Copyright © 1985 by Wendell Berry from *The Collected Poems of Wendell Berry, 1957–1982*. Reprinted by permission of Counterpoint.

"What I Should Have Said," by Terry Taylor, Copyright © 2000 Zoom Daddy Music, BMI. Used by permission.

EMOTIONAL WEATHER REPORT
Written by Tom Waits
©1975 Opus 19 Music (ASCAP)
Used By Permission. All Rights Reserved.

BETTER OFF WITHOUT A WIFE
Written by Tom Waits
©1975 Opus 19 Music (ASCAP)
Used By Permission. All Rights Reserved.

TAKE IT WITH ME
Written by Tom Waits and Kathleen Brennan
©1999 JALMA MUSIC (ASCAP)
Used By Permission. All Rights Reserved.

Wipf & Stock
An Imprint of Wipf and Stock Publishers
199 W. 8th Ave., Suite 3
Eugene, OR 97401
www.wipfandstock.com

ISBN 13: 978-1-60899-480-9

Manufactured in the U.S.A.

To Erika,

my wife, who, on more than one occasion, has locked the door behind me when I've stepped out to check the mail.

my wife, who asks me to hide the chocolate chips because she doesn't feel like she'll be strong enough to resist the temptation to snack on them and then, one day, has a chocolate craving so fierce she tears everything out of the kitchen drawers, everything off the shelves, everything out of the cupboards, just to try to find those damn chocolate chips.

my beautiful wife, whom I've watched use three different knives to cut up one apple. And then, when she was done, she put the slices into a cute bowl and walked away, leaving the knives—including the best knife, the go-to knife for everyday slicing and cutting, the German-made 6 inch paring knife that she gave to me for Christmas one year—the cut up apple core, and the apple juice, all sitting there on the cutting board, the knives getting sticky and the apple guts slowly turning brown.

my wife, my dearest friend in the whole world for the past seventeen years, who, as the very last thing she does before she goes to bed, takes one last look in the bathroom mirror and fixes her hair.

my wife, you are the soul of this book in all kinds of obvious ways, and in countless ways only you and I could know. I adore you.

Either life is holy with meaning,
    or life doesn't mean a damn thing.

—Frederick Buechner, "The Truth of Stories"

Contents

PART FOUR *LOVE IS A HOME*

Foreword

by Aiden Enns

My first significant encounter with Kurt Armstrong was through a piece of writing in *Geez* magazine, where I was working as an editor. Called, "To do this week," the article detailed the myriad imperatives to improve our lives.

He revealed the absurd level of daily obligations faced by well-meaning consumers: "Eat more leafy greens and fibrous vegetables. Eat fresh fruit. Eat only certified-organic fresh fruit. Eat only locally grown, certified-organic fresh fruit. Eat less carbs, less red meat, less chemical-saturated, processed junk food. Eat less. Eat either more or fewer eggs depending on what they tell you is healthier this month."

In Kurt's writing we see an amazing ability to observe and articulate, both of these are gifts to readers who yearn to understand and live meaningful lives in a culture strewn with banalities.

Following the publication of this article, Kurt, Erika, and their two kids, Molly and baby Jack, moved to the prairies and spent the next year crammed in a tiny, wood-heated, no-bedroom cabin. It was an experiment in living, about which he wrote for us several times. It was also, no doubt, a test of fire for their marriage.

In the dead of winter, my partner Karen and I drove out to visit this crazy homesteader and his family. I wanted to witness this exercise in living directly with the elements. I saw the fruit of a summer harvest in jars on a shelf near the ceiling and the fuel from the forest chopped and stacked outside their abode.

At that time, Kurt asked me how an eager writer might become an insider at *Geez* magazine. My response was simple, "Hang around and make yourself useful." Which is exactly what he did. The next year they moved to Winnipeg, and he eventually became a veteran on our team of section editors.

I was impressed with Kurt when I mentioned my anxiety of getting older and having few resources for retirement (by North American middle class standards we have a low income, plus we elected to have no children). "Aiden," he quickly replied, "you and Karen can come over and live with us. We'll take care of you." In the years since that seemingly flippant response, he's affirmed the sincerity of the offer and is now part of our community.

Kurt and I differ on many things. For example, we have different answers to questions about marriage, such as Who should get married to whom? and, Can we even redeem marriage from is patriarchal roots? But we agree on foundational things, such as the need for self-giving love (especially among men) and a commitment to work through conflict.

In a section on "the lonely terror of infinite choice," Kurt writes, "My self is not a finite resource of which I must be a cautious, stingy steward, but rather a gift I receive from others." Here and throughout the book he challenges the individualism and alienation reinforced in our consumer culture. Relationships are not products we consume, they are the occasion to manifest our capacity for love. They allow us to become who we are.

In this book and in his marriage to Erika, Kurt has shown us a patience and kindness that stems from love. I am encouraged by his yearning to be faithful to his partner for life and to the Christian tradition that binds them together. His journey, displayed here with such vulnerability, is honest, humble, and earnest. These qualities surely enrich any life and marriage.

Aiden Enns is editor of Geez *magazine and a sessional instructor at Canadian Mennonite University. Raised in Vancouver, he lives in Winnipeg, Manitoba, with Karen Schlichting, to whom he's been married for over twenty years.*

Sixteen

Myths about

Marriage

1. There is one person, somewhere out there, that you were destined for.

2. Everlasting bliss is possible if you find and marry that person.

3. Watch television dramas and sitcoms and lots of romantic-comedy movies to get an idea of what you're in for when you get married.

4. If your marriage is mediocre, you *must* get out of your marriage if you happen one day to meet that one person you were destined for.

5. Beauty generally determines the quality of the marriage: ugly people have ugly marriages, ordinary people have ordinary marriages, gorgeous people have gorgeous marriages, and movie stars have movie-star marriages.

6. For marriage to be blissful, a wife must be thin, busty, sweet, beautiful, and nubile. A husband can be anything—ugly, hairy, smelly, fat, annoying, and rude—just as long as he is wealthy, witty, occasionally sweet, and "good in bed."

7. Marriage is only one option, no better or worse than living together with your partner or having casual sex on a regular basis; but, should you choose to get married:

8. You *must* live together before you get married.

9. "Fidelity" has to do with stereo equipment.

10. Lasting romance and lots of sex are the essential ingredients that will keep your marriage alive.

11. Love has reasonable conditions and limits, much like your relationship with your auto mechanic: as long as you get what you want and the price is not too high, it doesn't hurt to stick with what you've got.

12. If you aren't having passionate, life-changing sex every time you're in bed together, something is wrong with the relationship, i.e. you probably married the wrong person, and you should consider getting a divorce.

13. When the romance is gone, so is the marriage, and you should get a divorce.

14. Marriage is supposed to satisfy your needs. It should not inhibit you from achieving your goals for your education, your career ambitions, and being all that you are meant to be, and if it ever does, you should get a divorce.

15. Prolonged, difficult, unresolved differences are best solved with a divorce.

16. Your first marriage can be considered a "starter marriage," a learning experience, and you should expect to get divorced at least once.

Introduction

Marriage

and

Consumer Culture

I want to overhear passionate arguments about what we are
and what we are doing and what we ought to do.

—Marilynne Robinson,
The Death of Adam

Unlike a lot of books, a new book on marriage
seems to require a *raison d'être*, some justification for adding yet another
volume to the jam-packed-and-growing "Relationships" section in the
bookstore. Mine is this: on the whole, marriage is taking a beating, and
I want to defend it.

Very nearly half of all marriages end in divorce, and Christian marriages are no exception. I've seen the statistic cited so frequently that it
doesn't surprise me anymore, and yet every time I hear of another friend
whose marriage has fallen apart, even if I'm not surprised, the truth
always hits me like a painful blow. Marriage is intimate, and marriage is
hard, damn hard. And our culture offers couples no meaningful encouragement to stay together through all the surprising, painful challenges
they run into, the inevitable (and necessary) harsh realities of marriage.
There are plenty of experts with plenty of advice, but not very many men
and women seem willing to speak honestly about difficulties of married
life, and journey alongside all of us non-experts.

It's easy to cite the usual explanations for our culture's rising divorce rate: a legal system that makes divorce easy and accessible, the rise of premarital cohabitation, the declining influence of traditional religious institutions, the seductive promises of sexual freedom in an increasingly promiscuous society. But I suspect that behind the widespread disintegration of marriage lies a deep crisis of meaning, a fundamental problem with our collective stories. Despite the postmodern undermining of the overarching metanarratives that have shaped and defined Western culture over the last five hundred years, we are still inheritors of stories great and small that help us locate ourselves individually and as a society. Whether we are always conscious of it or not, our culture tells stories that say where we've come from, who we are, and where we're going. And, as the postmodern critics have made abundantly clear, those stories have profound, far-reaching consequences for how we live.

The Christian wedding ritual celebrates marriage as a gift from God. Every Christian wedding ceremony has its roots in Genesis, where Adam and Eve are brought together by God to love one another, work together, and make a family. I take it on faith that marriage is still a gift, a distant descendant of that first couple, but it's not a blind faith: in the ongoing presence of my wife, I am reminded daily that marriage is a gift, the most beautiful, healing, transformative experience I have ever been given. It's better than I could have come up with on my own.

And harder, too. No doubt Adam and Eve's years together would have led to the usual unglamorous moments of everyday married life that all of us still face: drawn-out fights about little things and agonizing fights about big things, boredom, the temptation to break vows, the struggle to communicate openly, the challenges of sexual fidelity, disagreements over how to raise the kids, power struggles, hiding from intimacy, the ongoing effort to offer forgiveness and grace. Love isn't easy. No doubt the ongoing dynamics of even the best marriages include plenty of hard times, but marriage has always been that way, and it always will be. Marriage isn't meant to be easy; it's meant to be good. Marriage was God's idea from the start, and every marriage since Eden is an ongoing participation in God's original idea of marriage, a lifelong covenantal union characterized by active, engaged love, underwritten by grace, and charged with mystery.

Somewhere along the way in my early religious instruction, I got the impression that nothing good survived the cataclysmic fall of Genesis 3. Although things here on this earth might sometimes seem good, these could only be temptations of my sinful flesh or deceptions that the devil throws my way to distract me from the true eternal glory that I will only know when I reach heaven, Amen. But I'm no longer convinced of the "total depravity" of creation. What makes more sense to me is that the original goodness that God created in the Garden of Eden has survived the fall. In Genesis, we see the goodness of creation and we also see how sin entered the world, and from that point on through to the end of Revelation we get an ongoing description of how creation is the battleground for the cosmic war between God and evil. It doesn't say that when the sin came in, God packed up all that was good and put it away in a long-term, post-mortem celestial storage facility called Heaven. In Genesis, God pauses at the end of every day of creation to admire his work, and he can't seem to contain himself. Creation isn't good because God declares it so; God is making observations: "That crab apple tree is a fine piece of work, and that field of Ladyslippers is breathtaking. I really like those pronghorn antelope. Wow, that thunderstorm rumbling across that prairie landscape is breathtaking. And that man and woman down there falling in love— naïve, blissful, drunk on love—that's just what I had in mind, that's just right." His excitement is obvious: "Good, good," he says, over and over again, and when he gets to the end and makes man and woman, falling in love, he says, "*Very* good," and takes a day off to rest and enjoy it all. God is the one who first says, "It is <u>not</u> good for the man to be alone," and all of us ever since have felt the truth of that right down to our bones. From the very beginning we are truly made for one another. That longing for love is no illusion or deception; it's how we are meant to be.

I think we're in a period of deep confusion about what *marriage* is because we're confused about what *love* is. There's a lot of talk in Christian circles about our culture's view of things like sexuality, identity, gender roles, traditional values, and what legally constitutes a marriage, but I think some of our moralizing overlooks our deep misunderstanding of covenantal love, which is fundamental to marriage. Our confusion about the reality of love is largely due to the fact that covenantal love is in direct competition with the ubiquitous, seductive myths of consumer culture. Postmodern skepticism may have undermined the general mythological consensus of who we are and where we are going, but the ideology of the market has rushed in to fill the void. Though we have learned how to question hegemonic Western narratives like Christianity, Eurocentrism, science, and patriarchy, we are increasingly encouraged to think of ourselves fundamentally as consumers.

To describe our culture as a "consumer culture" is nothing new, but recognizing the ubiquitous force of consumerism and resisting its influence requires ongoing attention and effort. Consumerism as an ideology is a powerful and complex narrative with distinct values, assumptions, beliefs, and practices that set it in direct, irreconcilable opposition to true love. Consumerism says that the individual consumer is the center of meaning and everything that comes before each one of us—including our relationships—is an object of exchange that can ultimately be directed toward our satisfaction. Consumerism tells us that life is competitive and that love, just like every other valuable commodity, is scarce; that we must guard our interests, preserve our access to resources, and that we should be prepared to toss what we have when something newer and better comes along. We look for a love we think will suit us best, and expect to get just what we want. If we don't, we walk away. Choosing a relationship becomes no different than choosing a new car: we look at what's available, what seems interesting, what features we want, what style looks most interesting. I'm not trying to make an argument for or against a certain economic system, but when the values, beliefs, and practices of our culture's economic system are applied to our most intimate relationships, the results are uniformly destructive.

We live by our narratives, collective and individual, and the more we imbibe the stories of consumer culture, the more we come to live by them. The image-obsessed Hollywood story of passionate, romantic love pulls on us so strongly we start to wonder what's wrong with our own hum-drum love life; the happy, contented family in the car commercial turns into an ideal that we feel the need to emulate; the clean-shaven, muscular husband from the shaving cream ad and the breathless, seductive wife in the diamond necklace commercial define the roles and expectations of men and women and how spouses ought to display their love for one another.

The Christian narrative, which centers around the sacrificial, self-giving love of Jesus, is ultimately incompatible with the narrative of consumerism, but I think that a lot of us Christians have unconsciously located ourselves first and foremost in the narrative of consumer culture. This comes as no surprise. The ubiquitous messages and images of consumer culture are impossible to ignore and difficult to resist.

This is a book of passionate arguments and honest, true stories in defence of covenantal love. I want to expose the intoxicating consumerist assumptions we breathe in like air, and I want to find, instead, true, life-giving, meaning-filled stories for us to live and love by. I want to write honestly about what real-life marriage is like because I think the truth can shine some light on the sorts of lies that derail and destroy love. I want to tell personal stories of love, failure, confession, forgiveness, and renewal from my real life marriage as some alternatives to the commerce-driven stories that dominate our imagination and so profoundly mark the ways that we live. This book is my attempt to draw a direct line between the metaphors that shape our thinking and how we live our everyday lives and so recover the ancient practice of covenant.

A lot of the marriage books I've looked at try to make marriage seem straightforward, or they offer exaggerated promises based on secret knowledge or some special relational technique, and then provide supposedly straightforward steps for a husband and wife to follow to achieve some magical, otherworldly relationship. Psychologists, therapists, medical experts, relationship gurus, sociologists, and theologians all have something to say about marriage, and much of it makes not a stitch of difference in my relationship with my wife. Without question, we can benefit from some of the observations and discoveries of experts, but at the end of the day we need more than the research, statistics, and imperatives of specialists lobbed at us from a safe, clinical distance. We need loving testimony from men and women who are wholeheartedly engaged with the real-life stuff of marriage because marriage is essentially the layperson's business. Marriage requires the ongoing, willed practice of love, and just like learning to play a musical instrument, simply wanting to be good at it doesn't accomplish much. There is no substitute for time spent practicing. There are no shortcuts. No amount of expert advice can get us out of the hard work of marriage, and most husbands and wives are everyday people who are painfully aware that they don't really know what they're doing, that they've stepped onto the stage in a play they know very little about. "We are called to no rehearsals, only public performances," says Robert Farrar Capon. "Everything that matters has to be read at sight."[1] Husbands and wives are all amateurs in the truest sense of the word: marrying and living together through whatever life throws our way, *for the love of it.* I don't put much stock in the techniques or step-by-step programs because in the end, after the books are highlighted, the seminars wrapped up, and the counseling sessions completed, it's still the everyday decisions of everyday people living their everyday lives that provides the soil for the kind of strong, particular marriages worthy of our attention. I can tell you that my marriage isn't perfect, but that's a silly, hollow confession because a "perfect" marriage doesn't exist. Perfection implies completion, and our marriages are only ever completed or "accomplished" by a funeral. You can only say that you have finally "succeeded" at being married when you have stayed faithful in love until one of you dies. In marriage, death is the peculiar finishing mark of success.

So here I am, an amateur husband, ten years into marriage, and my relationship with Erika is more surprising, fresh, and mysterious than it has ever been, as strong as the great elm tree in front of our house. I don't know any rules about how to fix marriages or a formula for how to make them work, but I have tried to observe marriage closely, look at it from different angles and in varying shades of light. I haven't figured it out, but I doubt that anyone else has either, not even the experts. In a decade of married life, I have discovered that I am susceptible to the same self-made traps that destroy other people's marriages—resentment, pride, lust, envy, betrayal, selfishness, distrust, greed, unkindness, jealousy, bitterness—some more than others. But in spite of all that, my marriage is somehow healthy, life-giving, surprising, beautiful, consoling, comforting, and challenging, growing stronger every day. Thankfully, marriage is only for imperfect people. If I can do it, I suspect that just about anyone can.

1. Capon, "An Offering of Uncles," 127.

If mapping out a kind of technical user's manual for marriage, with goals, steps, and techniques, as though it were some kind of machine, betrays the poetic truth of marriage, then the opposite danger of not being concrete enough leads to dreamy, esoteric images of a disembodied ideal that make marriage seem like something best experienced in a trance-like state. God, save us from the champions of the mystical marriage! Marriage is for humans, not angels. We are physical beings, loving our husband or wife in all the commonplace details of day-to-day existence. Marriage, like life itself, is indeed a mystery, but it is inescapably fleshy. It only exists here in this world of sight, sound, touch, smell, and taste. Warning us against the temptation towards escapist, otherworldly spirituality, Scott Cairns writes:

> I think that you
> forget the very issue which
> induced the Christ to take on flesh.
>
> All loves are bodily, require
> that the lips part, and press their trace
> of secrecy upon the one
>
> beloved— [2]

Marriage takes place with our bodies, which we so often think of as burdens rather than extraordinary, exquisite gifts. But we do not *have* bodies: we *are* bodies. Nothing, except perhaps death itself, is a more poignant testimony to the significance of our bodiliness than marriage. The search for the deeper mysteries of marriage is a dangerous distraction if it carries our imagination away from this world and toward some unreal, disembodied ideal. Marriage should draw our attention ever closer to that which is right before us, this lover of flesh and bone, this most intimate other. As the poetic novelist and wise essayist Marilynne Robinson says, "With all respect to heaven, the scene of miracle is here, among us."[3] This plunge into the miracle and mystery of marriage is not an escape from this world; it's a headfirst dive into the deep end of fleshy physicality. And such an intimate encounter with mystery and miracle can never happen by buying some new and novel product, as the advertisers would have us believe. No, there is more to marriage than we will ever comprehend, but we can

2. Cairns, "Loves," 161–62.
3. Robinson, "Psalm Eight," 243.

learn to live in wonder at the wholly human other, the man or woman before us.

Even as I have tried to find clarity as I put my thoughts into words, I've done more than just chronicle what has happened in my marriage. In writing, my senses have been awakened, and I have cultivated a deeper sense of wonder at this mystery of marriage—so rich, marvelous, and endlessly surprising, this grace that keeps overflowing from my life with Erika. I write to defend my particular, strong, fragile, and vulnerable love in a world that gives no honor to the kind of faithfulness and commitment that marriage requires. And at the same time I want to share these reflections with anyone who is interested, to encourage them to discover these mysteries for themselves. If I fail to give a faithful account, it is certainly not for having been given too little.

PART
ONE

Body and Soul

Brought to My Senses

CHAPTER 1

SIGHT

Molly is in bed for the night, and Erika is out with friends at her Monday night meeting. My mind is wandering. I'm anxious, though not about anything in particular.

Though we rarely watch TV, tonight I haul it out of the closet and set it up on the shelf in the bedroom. I hook up the old wire antenna and string it around the room to try to get a clear picture. I can usually pick up six channels—four of them are in English—depending on how I hang the antenna and whether or not the people upstairs are using certain kitchen appliances at the time. But I'm hardly "watching" anything here: I don't stick with any one thing for more than a couple of minutes. I flip from the local news, to a sitcom with an unconvincing laugh-track, to some "reality" show about pop singers, to a crime drama about a new murder this week, and it all starts to blur. I don't stay on a program long enough to even catch a story line. The advertisements exhaust me: thirty-second rapid-fire comedies or dramas, and watching them reminds me why we keep the TV in the closet. I had imagined that a bit of mindless time with television would be a relaxing treat, but now I'm even more restless than I was an hour ago.

But I keep watching anyway, flipping between channels, hoping I might find something to capture my attention. I can waste hours doing this, watching nothing, gazing at the flashing blue light, gawking at every gadget and gizmo splayed, hawked, and dressed up to look like something I need, and I don't even understand why I'm watching because I'm conscious of the fact that I am truly wasting my time, and the longer I sit here, the more my mental "To Do" list starts to feel like a bee stinging my conscience—I should do the dishes and I still need to write that film review and I owe Walter a letter and I still haven't fixed the shelves downstairs and I need to weed the garden and fix the drywall at the neighbors' place and work on my resume and there's no doubt I need to start eating better and I need to get more exercise. But I just sit.

Then I hear a key in the lock, the first of a string of familiar sounds, those of Erika coming home: the front door banging shut, folding of an umbrella, click and squeak of closet doors—one for coats, the other for boots—footsteps towards the bedroom. I turn off the TV, awakened not by an image or style, but by a real presence. Her cheeks are red from the cold. She smiles at me. I feel sheepish for wasting the evening, but my wasting time doesn't bother her. She lays down beside me, puts her arm across my shoulders and rests her head on my chest like she's listening to my heart. I look at her face. Every so often when I see her face—at a glance before she notices, or examining her closely, as I do now—it almost feels like I am seeing her for the first time. She is still strange to me. I have known her half my life, but when I close my eyes, I can hardly picture her face, as though the longer I know her the more mysterious she becomes.

We undress and climb into bed, and she turns out the light.

SOUND

My workday starts when the alarm clock squawks at 5 am. I get up and make some toast, being careful not to set off the smoke alarm. I ride my bike to work on quiet streets, the city just starting to rev up to speed—delivery trucks, a van, transit busses, a few cars with commuters. There's a siren wailing up the street behind me, but it turns onto a side street.

When I get to work, the music is thumping. Customers show up, order, and wait. I command the big coffee grinder and the hissing espresso machine that seems as big as a little Italian car, and serve up expensive lattes and cappuccinos. A couple hours into my shift, the morning rush arrives, and the banter with the regulars is comfortable and predictable: clichés about work, weather, and politics, gossip from the tabloids, bits of bad news from the day's newspaper. I holler names and drinks, but it's hard to be heard over the din of waiting customers and the steady rumble of the coffee roaster in the corner of the room. The satellite radio continuously pipes in a stream of banal songs that all blend together, one into the next. When I started working here, I used to get the songs stuck in my head and they would play on like a jukebox when I was trying to fall asleep at night. Now I hardly notice the music at all. Outside, the cars and busses hiss by on the wet streets.

I'm done by early afternoon. The mid-morning rain has passed and I bike home down the crowded streets: more cars, trucks, vans, busses, sirens, and lots of horns. Vancouver drivers love to use their horns.

When I open the door, I hear Molly shaking a rattle, jangling a bell, and blowing a whistle all at once. "Hi, daddy," she says. Erika asks me about my day, and I tell her, then ask how the two of them have been. I put on a record, and Molly and I dance together for the first song. I can hear the city workers outside—tractors, dump trucks, jackhammers, cement saws. They're replacing the water system and they've peeled back the asphalt, like they're doing surgery on the city's arteries.

Erika and I start working on supper, while Molly stacks blocks and then crashes her little towers with a toy car. Erika and I scrub and peel, slice, chop, and dice meat and vegetables. I whisk a sauce, and she fries the meat. Molly whines and fusses, so I give her a little cup of raisins to snack on until supper is ready. Supper sizzles and simmers, bubbles and boils.

Just when it's ready and we are about to sit down to eat, the phone rings. "Sorry," Erika says without answering it, "it's suppertime here." Molly eats almost everything we feed her and throws the rest on the floor, laughing and doing her best to hold our attention throughout the meal. The phone rings again; we ignore it. Molly throws her cup on the floor and squeals when I give her a bowl of grapes for dessert. She complains when I clean her fingers and face. We clean up the dishes, put the leftovers in the fridge. Erika transfers a load of wet laundry to the dryer. Molly giggles when I tickle her and wrestle with her on the bed, whines when I change her diaper, fusses when I put her into her pyjamas, and asks me to sing to her when I brush her teeth. In the bathroom, I can overhear the owner of the house, talking in a high, squeaky baby voice to her dog. Downstairs, Erika starts the washing machine.

Molly gives us goodnight kisses, and we put her down in her playpen. I call my brother on the phone, and we talk about books, kids, movies, our marriages, our parents. He tells me that the squealing metal of the trains in the train yard near his house is starting to make him feel like he's going crazy. "The sound of it," he says, "I hear it in the middle of the night. It keeps me awake. It makes me so angry. Maybe we'll just have to move, I don't know." I tell him how we used to live right next to one of the busiest streets in the city, and how I had to sleep with earplugs because the incessant noise of the vehicles kept me awake. "That's part of the reason we moved to this place," I tell him, "the noise and all."

Erika and I pick up Molly's toys and get ready for bed. Everything is tidied up for tomorrow. We get into bed and talk for a bit about the day, the joys and struggles, the big dreams of our life. We tell each other how in love we are with Molly, plan our schedule for the next day, and can hardly keep our eyes open. She switches off the lamp and kisses me goodnight.

And tonight happens to be one of those rare nights when she falls asleep before I do. I listen to her slow, deep breaths, the faint whistling from her nose, the sound of her *life*. I fall asleep to the rhythm of her breathing in, breathing out, breathing in, breathing out. Breathing.

TOUCH

At the bus stop this morning, there's a giant picture of an anonymous woman's bra-clad torso. The lighting and computer-enhanced color tints make everything look too good to be true, which, of course, it is. Like a lot of men, even though I can offer sound moral and philosophical arguments for why a bus stop advertisement featuring a lacy bra on a faceless torso should be offensive, more than anything, I want to stare. I think of the lines from one of Wendell Berry's poems:

> How hard it is for me, who live
> in the excitement of women
> and have the desire for them
> in my mouth like salt.[1]

When the bus pulls up, the ad on the side portrays a man and woman, both half-dressed, the two of them a tangle of limbs. They both look tired or drunk, and both of them are sweaty. Just before the bus doors open, I notice that the ad is actually for shoes, or rather a shoe company.

On the bus there are ads for hair and skin products, for natural cures with miraculous before-and-after photos, and clothing stores. There's a confusing "safe sex" poster that seems like attempted damage control, conspicuously out of place, I muse, like a bandaid over a bullet wound, or a 1-800 gambling addiction hotline number printed on the seats at a casino.

And on the inside roof, like the advertiser's centrepiece, is a photo of another anonymous woman from the waist up, who is looking down at the cell phone-shaped opening in her shirt that shows off a section of her bra and an ample amount of cleavage. I have seen this ad before, and I try not to stare, but the whole point of it is that I do stare, and that hopefully the curve of her breasts will entice me into buying a cell phone. When I get off the bus, I see a billboard advertising the "Naughty But Nice" sex tradeshow—no doubt a gratuitous carnival of images, fantasies, desires, and obsessions. But the allure is powerful and real. I can't pretend I am not drawn to the images, so carefully created and displayed, and my mind starts to wander. I walk home, feeling like there's something wrong with me.

That night, Erika and I make love.

I know her body. I know the lines and veins, the scar on her foot, the one under her chin, the one on her shin from a cut with a clamshell, the stretch-marked skin around her hips. I know the different tints and lines in her hair, the smooth curve of her neck, her soft earlobes, the pale, smooth skin on her shoulders and stomach and

---

1. Berry, "Marriage," 70.

back. I know her teeth—some straight, some crooked—and her nose, narrow like that of a Russian princess, her pointy chin, the creases that frame her mouth, her green eyes, different from when we first fell in love—traced by deeper lines and wrinkles, signs that she is being transformed by sorrow and joy.

I've covered every inch of her with my eyes and fingers, thousands of times now, over and over, and still she is new, every time, new. I look for some easier way to apprehend her, some way to make her more mine, but there is nothing simple about her body. Touching her is a mystery of flesh and bone. The real presence of her body resists the smallness of my eyes, my mind, all the words I use to describe her. She *is*.

Tacit Knowledge

and the Miraculous

Double Ristretto

I didn't really develop a serious appetite for books until midway through my second year of college. I remember sitting on the stools between the library shelves in Bible school, discovering Nietzsche—who got me all worked up—and Thomas Merton—who helped calm me down—and thinking that books like these were so explosive I could hardly believe they were legal. Reading has become so much a part of my life that nowadays I panic if I'm on the bus or in the waiting room at the doctor's office and discover that I've forgotten to bring along at least one of the half-dozen or so books I currently have on the go. In fact, I enjoy reading so much I can even think of a few reasons why it might be better than sex: the pleasures of reading might not be as intense as the pleasures of sex, but regardless of how good a lover you might be, chances are pretty good that a good book is going to last a whole lot longer than even the best sex; it's easy to talk to your kids about books; you can read in pretty much any public place without having to worry about getting arrested.

Not long ago I was reading from *Bodies in Motion and at Rest* by Thomas Lynch, a lifelong undertaker who also writes poetry and essays. The essay I was reading was about the author and his son fishing together. After only a few paragraphs, it was obvious just how much the two of them love fishing—not just catching fish, which would seem to be the obvious goal of anyone who goes fishing, but the entire experience of fishing, the sheer *physicality* of it all. Writing about his son, Lynch says, "It was here the topography of the riverbed began to make sense to him. He could close his eyes and see the bottom, its undulant waterscape of runs and pools and holes and flats, the pockets of curling water, the structure of tree stumps and rock forms, the gravel beds where fish would hold, the shaded and the sunlit waters."[1]

"He could close his eyes and see the bottom." That is, of course, literally nonsense: close your eyes and you can't see anything at all. But those lines suggest a very real way of knowing that has everything to do with the wonder of bodies, something Lynch ponders a great deal as he goes about his odd vocational pairing of undertaker and poet. I can picture Lynch and his son in their hip-waders, standing in a stream, their feet on the bottom, bodies balancing against the current, watching the surface of the water while feeling for the subtle movements that would begin at the fly tied to the end of the line and travel down the line floating on the river's surface and then up to the pole and down to their hands, their fishing rods extensions of their arms. Neither of them has actually seen the bottom of this stream, but Lynch says that his son could "see" what the bottom of the stream looked like by experiencing those subtle movements.

Lynch's description reminds me of philosopher Michael Polanyi's description of something he calls "tacit knowledge." Polanyi uses the metaphor of a walking stick to develop his philosophy of knowledge: "As we learn to use a probe, or to use a stick for feeling our way," he writes, "our awareness of its impact on our hand is transformed into a sense of its point touching the objects we are exploring . . . We become aware of the feelings in our hand in terms of their meaning located at the tip of the probe or stick to which we are attending."[2] In Lynch's essay, the fishing rod is the probe that very nearly becomes an extension of the fisherman's arm, and in turn, an extension of his eye, a way of

1. Lynch, "Fish Stories," 153–54.
2. Polanyi, *The Tacit Dimension*, 13.

seeing. His fishing rod is a tool, not just for catching fish, but for exploration. The knowledge Lynch and his son receive from their fishing rods, however, is different from a scientific knowledge based on measurements of the velocity of the current, underwater erosion, the viscosity of fluids, and the different grades of pebbles, sand, and silt that one could use to accurately describe the bottom of this streambed. It speaks of a knowing that is inseparable from physical, involved, active love, and it is as real as anything about which science can speak.

Now I'm not much of an outdoorsman, and it must be nearly twenty years since I last went fishing, and that may be why reading that essay got me thinking about coffee rather than my limited experience as an angler. I used to work at one of the top-rated coffee shops in Vancouver where I served espresso drinks for more than three years, and pulling double shots of espresso required a similar kind of knowing that involved both my *body* and *love*.

At work, we used to quietly poke fun at Starbucks coffee because everything about it seemed too easy: overcooked, pre-ground, pre-packaged beans, dispensed, dispersed, and disposed of with the push of a button labeled "PUSH" (presumably for the technically challenged). At our café, we used top of the line coffee grinders and espresso machines, and operating them well required some basic training, attention to detail, and, more than anything, tons of practice. My job taught me to pay attention to my body and my senses; to smell, touch, sight, sound, and, of course, taste, all of which were required to do the work well. The hours I spent learning to make a perfect double espresso or a perfect traditional cappuccino taught me about my body and helped me learn to love being a body.

Let me give you a simple and seemingly irrelevant example: when someone ordered a drink, I could grab a cup from one of the upside-down stacks of eight, twelve, and sixteen ounce paper cups—the bottom of the cup at the top of the tall pile—and hold it between my thumb and middle finger, tight enough that I wouldn't drop it, but loose enough so that as I brought my hand over to the espresso machine I could flip the cup right-side up and slide it down into the palm of my hand. I adjusted my grip ever so slightly, depending on the size of the cup. A small thing in a day's work, but it became a source of wonder. I learned to love that little trick, even though no one else ever noticed it—the sweeping motion, the movements of my arm, hand and fingers, the elementary Newtonian physics behind it all. It wouldn't be impossible to make a machine that could do it for you, but it will always be impossible to make a machine that could enjoy it. That I could do it just so was because I'd picked up something like 250,000 or so paper cups during the three years I worked there, every single one of them requiring my body, my senses of sight and touch, and a deepening non-scientific understanding of some basic principles of mass, gravity, and air friction that lay behind my little trick.

Another example: making espresso, the capital-c of Coffee, Sweet Black Gold, The Blessed Sap. A perfect espresso ristretto is a true delicacy, an ounce and a half of liquid miracle. I am sure that it must be one of a handful of drinks that God had in mind when he invented tastebuds. The perfect espresso shot always starts with the precise amount of fresh coffee ground at just the right coarseness—too fine and it will come out tasting burnt and bitter, too coarse and it's sour and mean, the margin between those two being very narrow—added to the hot espresso portafilter. I would tap that full portafilter on the edge of the grinder to loosely pack the grounds, one, two, three times, and then sweep my index and middle fingers back and forth, back and forth, back and forth, back and forth, levelling the ground coffee, making sure there were no empty pockets and that the ground coffee was an even, loosely packed "puck." (Could an automated, high-tech machine possibly appreciate the rich aroma of the coffee at that very moment? Could that machine ever make sense of the subtle adjustments I would make to the coarseness of the grind, depending on the time of day, whether there's sunshine or rain, the changes in the air temperature, whether the back door in the kitchen is open or closed, whether the espresso is two days old or six days old? Could a machine ever truly "know" these things? More importantly, could it ever care?)

Next step: tamping the ground coffee. First tamp—line up the tamper in the portafilter, straighten arm and lock wrist, and lean in. *Hard.* Thirty-five pounds pressure is what the training manual suggested, but I know I tamped harder. My co-worker Krista told me she tested her tamp using a bathroom scale, and it was about eighty pounds of pressure. Mine was less—maybe sixty-five? Seventy? Lift the tamper, then tamp again. Lift, and tamp again, but this time it's less about actually packing the coffee and more about "polishing" the top of the ground coffee by spinning the tamper. And it really does look polished. Not shiny, but like a water-worn stone. Beautiful.

Last step: hold the portafilter handle and with a quick flip of the wrist, toss away any loose grinds, while the tamped coffee puck remains intact. Reassemble the portafilter into the espresso machine—basically a glorified kettle—and watch the hot water work its magic. I developed a good sense of how the espresso would taste by looking at the streams as they flowed: if I'd done it right, the espresso would start with slow drips after two or three seconds, suddenly speed up into golden brown streams like burnt butter for about twenty seconds or so, and then just as the streams began to run light and thin, I'd shut the machine off. In the porcelain demitasse, you would see a layer of the thick, golden *crema*, flecked with auburn, floating on top of the strong, pitch-black, sweet, pure coffee. Sometimes it seemed that no matter what I did I couldn't get my espresso shots to turn out right. But most times it would work *perfectly*, a satisfying conjunction of touch, sight, sound, smell, and last of all—*taste*.

Most of us go about our work life and everyday business without a whole lot of dreamy, philosophical contemplation of our corporeal existence. As one who so loves to read, it's sometimes easy for me to live as though my body is an inconvenience, as though I am a mind trapped in a burdensome body, but every now and then something unusual—it could be very profound or very everyday—can spark a sense of wonder at bodies: the moments when my children were born; or seeing my brother-in-law lay a perfect course of bricks, or the feel of a sharp knife slicing through potatoes from the garden, or stepping outside at night in the biting winter, Winnipeg air, or pulling a double-shot of espresso, or reading an undertaker's thoughts on fishing—all of these stir in me a sense of wonder and fascination at the basic fact of bodily existence. "Our body is the ultimate instrument of all our external knowledge, whether intellectual or practical," writes Polanyi. "Our own body is the only thing in the world which we normally never experience as an object, but experience always in terms of the world to which we are attending from our body."[3] Like the sweet taste of a double shot of espresso, Polanyi and Lynch help to remind me that I don't just *have* a body: I *am* a body. *Wow — same thought*

We don't much believe in miracles anymore. Mostly we trust that science and math can offer quantifiable, rational, empirical explanations for all the things that once seemed so mysterious. Science and math, we are told, have carried us beyond the need for a miracle. I, however, have my doubts. Starbucks, I think, is science and math. Starbucks has taken the miracle of golden espresso streaming into a warm, porcelain demitasse and made it into an equation, the outcome being a predictably hot, milky beverage with caffeine and a measured squirt of some artificial, seasonally appropriate flavored sweetener—pumpkin pie or cinnamon, maybe—to mask any possible bitterness. Ordering your drink at Starbucks is easy, and you can expect your drink to be served quickly. The goal is to inspire warm, sentimental feelings, repeat customers, and brand loyalty, but only in the most unusual and exceptionally rare case could it ever inspire something like genuine love.

But great coffee—capital-c Coffee—requires *sensual* people, bodies that are attentive to taste, touch, and smell, fleshy human beings doing the kind of work that no machine will ever do: love. All of this strikes me as fundamentally miraculous, not just because coffee tastes so good, but because it is there at all. That good espresso exists—that anything exists—brings us into the direct glare of the fundamental miracle of being, the very thing that inspired even the curmudgeonly atheist Edward Abbey to write: "To me the most mysterious thing about the universe is not its comprehensibility but the fact that it exists. And the same mystery attaches to everything within it. The world is permeated through and through with mystery."[4] The world is here when there might just as well have been nothing at all—no coffee plants, nobody to run the roasters, no espresso machines, no you, no me, nothing—but here it is anyways, a perfect double-shot, and here I am, enjoying the smell of it, and there you are, reading about it. Big Bang or big-c Creation, take your pick, but here we are, billions of years after the fact, and I'm sitting here with a glass of cold water and a demitasse of double-shot house espresso that my friend just served me, and judging by the smell and look of it, it's going to be good. I call that miraculous.

Little things, of course, but then almost all of life is made up of precisely those sorts of little things, and if we spend all of our time waiting around for the big things, we'll end up missing nearly ev-

4. Abbey, "Watching, the Birds: The Windhover," 51.

erything. So Thank God, I say! Thank God for coffee beans, for the farmers who grow them, and the fires that roast them. Thank God for the engineers who design the grinders, and the friction that turns roasted beans into freshly ground coffee. Thank God for boiling water, gravity, taste buds, and for the ongoing miracle of long-chain carbon molecules that make that double ristretto taste so damn good.

The

Insufficient

Self

CHAPTER 3

For as long as I can remember, I have always been falling in love.

When I was four I fell in love with Carolyn, the prettiest girl I'd ever seen. Her parents were good friends of my parents, so it felt like destiny that we should be together. I remember visiting them once with my mom, while Carolyn was at school (thus marking the beginning of my lifelong pursuit of older women), but I could tell by looking at her straight brown hair, dark brown eyes and inviting smile in the school photo above her parents' stereo that she was my kind of girl. In my head I called her my girlfriend—until I got to grade one and fell in love with Kim, who was seventeen. *her*.

In grade three, Becky came to spend a week with my older sister after summer camp ended, and she fell in love with *me*. She told my sister she thought I was a "totally gorgeous hunk of a babe," and that she'd go out with me whenever I was ready. I didn't know what "going out" or "hunk of a babe" meant. The only hunks I knew were hunks of dirt we lobbed around the garden, pretending they were grenades. It was the first time a girl had ever liked me, but I don't think I ever talked to her, and after she left I couldn't remember what she looked like. So I pictured me and a made-up version of her going for quiet walks together around our farm, strolling in the summer sun, jumping on the trampoline, and laughing like we were part of a Disney movie. She lived three hours away, and I never saw her or heard from her again, but that didn't stop me from calling her my girlfriend for more than a year.

My cousin Dan and his family moved to our farm when I was in grade five, and we went to school together for the year that they stayed. He started writing love notes to Marion, and because Dan was pretty much my best friend, I decided that I really liked her too. But his handwriting was neat and mine was small and scribbly and hard to read. She chose Dan, and I tried not to be jealous.

By junior high the hormones hit like a flood, and I started falling in love every day. I had crushes on every single one of my sister's friends, sometimes all at once. They were a year older and therefore more mysterious and beautiful than the girls in my grade, but not one of them showed me any attention. I aimed higher. I had crushes on the girls all the way up to grade twelve. No luck. I was tall for my age, but I was pimply, gangly, and awkward, my cracking voice stuck ambiguously between boy and man, and despite my best preventative efforts I always had a foot odor problem. On top of that, I was only twelve. *ha*

But then I met Lana at the week-long co-ed summer camp my church sponsored. She was tall, thin, and had puppy dog eyes hidden behind a curtain of hairspray-crusted bangs. She was shy and very quiet, and I was nervous around her, but during meals and at chapel I always tried to sit close enough that I could smell her perfume. When our paths crossed I tried to catch her eye by making a strange face or doing a ridiculous dance. I thought if I could make her laugh she would like me. At the end of the week, I got her address. We wrote letters for *wow* nearly a year, one or two a week, and we saw each other when our youth groups got together for special events. When she turned fifteen, I asked her out in a letter, and she wrote me back and said yes, so I bought her a ticket to see Michael W. Smith in concert. My mom drove us to the city and Lana and I sat in the back seat holding hands. I got my very first kiss on the drive home, but two weeks later she dumped me and never told me why.

In high school I went to weekend youth retreats and fell in love every time. At one of them, the guest speaker talked about eternal relationships and earthly relationships, describing how important it was for us to make sure that above all else, we ought to have a right relationship with God. "He wants your whole life, not just the Sundays," he said. He told us about his life when he was our age, how he had dated tons of girls, but he had never found the satisfaction he was looking for. "I thought I was looking for love," he said, "but what I was really looking for was Jesus. You've got to get things right with God before you go falling in love with someone, or you'll end up no further ahead than when you started. You've got to be satisfied with your relationship with God, just you and him, just the two of you, before you're ready to be dating someone. If you aren't satisfied on your own, you're not ready to date."

It made me feel guilty about how much I liked girls, but it fit with my understanding of what God wanted and what I owed him. I couldn't expect to find any sort of satisfying love in someone else because God was the only one who could give me what I needed most. Just me and Jesus, that would be enough, and until I could figure out how to be satisfied on my own, trying to find a girlfriend would be a distraction. By the time I got to college, I still felt the burning hunger for soul-filling love, but I never forgot that I was not yet whole, that I was not in a relationship with God where he satisfied my every longing. I thought that if I did fall in love with someone, God would take her away from me so I would learn to depend completely on him first. The message lingered: get everything right between God and yourself, and only then will you be spiritually ready for the kind of romantic relationship God wants you to have.

The encouragement to be content on one's own is probably a necessary antidote to the kind of illusions that fill romantic comedies, where love really does make everything turn out nicely, so sweet, perfect and whole. But the fact is, we will never be whole. We are all restless, hungry, broken, unfinished, incomplete souls. Sometimes that sense of being unfinished can keep us moving ahead, keep us alive, drive us to pursue whatever it is that we feel we might be missing; sometimes the needs and longings are deep and crippling, like bleeding, open wounds. But however severe our brokenness, we're all trying to get healed. Healing—becoming more fully human—is always incomplete.

If we hold out for perfection, not only will we be perpetually discontent by always being less than whole, but we will also never come to terms with our own fallibility, shortcomings and brokenness. Life itself is an unfinished business, and being human comes with a lifelong search for wholeness. There are no shortcuts, no quick fixes, no prayer or incantation to make everything alright.

The idea that we should be completely right with God before we're ready for a relationship perpetuates the same myth of the perfect self that romantic comedies do. The romantic comedy says that we become perfectly whole and satisfied *when* we fall in love with just the right person; the me-and-Jesus version says, "I'll bring my completed, perfect self to your completed, perfect self and together we can have the happiest marriage anyone has ever had, God bless us both." In both cases, the perfect, self-sufficient, self-reliant man or woman is still the ultimate goal.

This ideal of the detached, perfect self is an inheritance of a version of God as detached, static and unchanging—a deity who more closely resembles the ideal Greek philosopher than the God who created us to be in relationship with others. In Genesis, we don't learn exactly how God created the world, but we do find out why: God creates out of abundance and overflowing love, not detached perfection. The Christian God is not a cold, stand-offish cosmic intellectual; he is continuously, actively involved with the whole of creation, from the infinitely small to the incomprehensibly large, and everything in between, including all of us and the incomplete self each of us has to offer.

I have tried to find comfort and satisfaction in God alone, striving for the "just me and Jesus" ideal, but the experiences of divine comfort I've felt have been very sporadic. I have found the greatest satisfaction and comfort in my relationships with others. I don't believe life-giving relationships with others and faith in God are mutually exclusive. The life-giving time I spend with my close friends is not something I find *instead* of finding God; it is *from* God, a gift that is a part of his active, ongoing love. God is present to me through the deep bonds I have with friends and family; he comforts me time and again through things like conversations, shared meals, shared work, common worship, and times spent in silence with other fallible, incomplete people. Longing for an unmediated encounter with God alone makes me overlook the gifts of love that are right before me, waiting to embrace me.

After I graduated from college I went on a backpacking trip to Morocco, driven by a desperate hunger for God, whom I hoped I would meet in some mystical way while I was there. The destination was inspired by an issue of National Geographic, but the trip itself was inspired by the writings of fourth-century Desert Fathers and Mothers. Before I bought my ticket I had a dream that I rode on a bus to the middle of the desert and met God.

Morocco was the only "big trip" I had ever taken and I went alone. I thought I would be fine, comforted by God's presence, but it was the loneliest time of my life. I spent the first three anxious days wandering around the streets of Casablanca, kicking through the trash in the gutter, looking for some sense of self, some trace of God. For two weeks I dreamed every night that I was back in Canada. I wished for some tragedy back home that would give me a reason, other than cowardice, to return to my family. By the end of my second week, I started to feel like a traveler, and over the next month and a half I traveled 5000 miles of roads and railways. I visited Marrakech, Meknes, Fez, and the Atlas Mountains; I wandered through the ruins of an ancient Roman outpost, drove through rocky, desolate valleys, and stayed in a $3 a night hotel room that overlooked the Atlantic. And I spent days and nights in the Sahara, just like in my dream, but I never did have any mystical, solitary encounter with God, never felt that singular divine embrace I was looking for. But I did find love as others took me in and fed me, cared for me, gave me a bed to sleep in, and blessed me as I went on my way. Once, I was invited to a lunch with a devout Muslim family of twelve. We crowded around a small table and for three hours we shared platters of olives, bread, lamb, chicken, and vegetables that we ate with our hands. Another time, a young teacher stopped me and asked to talk so he could practice his English. I met up with him again later in my trip, and he invited me to stay in his family's home. Those strangers shared love, God's love.

My Morocco trip was in the middle of my "locust years," the half-decade after college when I was still in love with Erika, even though we weren't together. I remember telling my younger brother that it was good for me to be alone for a while. I knew I had plenty of problems that I needed to get right in my own life—struggles, wounds, sins, failures, things that I thought I should get right before I was ready to be in a relationship again. "I'm sorry, but that's nonsense," he said. "If you wait to fall in love until you 'get it together,' you'll never get married. You'll always be a more-or-less broken, messed up version of yourself, and waiting to become perfect is only waiting to become someone else."

Years later, on our first real date after five years apart, Erika took me out for supper, and I told her that I wanted to be with her, but that I had a lot of things to sort before I was ready for a relationship. I said I needed time on my own to deal with my problems. I was anxious, uncertain about who I was and what I wanted, and often very depressed. My faith was shallow, misguided and confused. I felt like an inadequate mess. She said she understood. But my warnings didn't scare her away. She loved me anyway and decided to keep after me, and within a year we were married, two more inadequate, incomplete people, binding themselves together with the promise to love one another through to the very end.

It doesn't take perfect people to make a marriage work. The problems that we carry with us into marriage don't go away on their own, and marriage doesn't make them go away either. The man or woman who vows to be with you until death, the one who learns to see you more clearly than you see yourself, becomes like a mirror, showing you your self-defeating, sinful ways of living, and then offering you the love you need to find healing. In the crucible and covenant of marriage, we are free to expose the wounds of our souls without the fear of being rejected or asked to keep quiet and go away until we get better. I am more me, more whole because of my marriage to Erika—not because I have worked so hard at being a better person, but because marriage has been a safe place for me to be healed and become more fully alive. Anyone who hopes that marriage will be the cure for brokenness or provide ultimate and final satisfaction will certainly be disappointed; likewise anyone who avoids marriage on the basis of their own shortcomings will never be well enough to get married. Everyone who enters the covenant of marriage, knowing that they are fallible, broken, and incomplete, promising to offer and receive love as a place to heal and to be healed, will find what they need.

The Lonely

Terror of

Infinite Choice

From childhood onward, most of us have been told how important it is to "just be yourself." Shakespeare's, "To thine own self be true," from *Hamlet*, is routinely plucked out of context and transformed into poetic wisdom, encouraging restless, angst-ridden teenagers to press on in their quest to find out who they really are. "Be yourself," "Believe in yourself," "Be true to yourself"—by the time I was in my twenties I had heard it so many times in so many different contexts that it never occurred to me that there were any other real options. But before I could ever *be* myself I needed something solid to identify as the *self* I was supposed to be.

In junior high I knew that I needed to figure out some way to balance being myself with the equal but opposite need to fit in. There were kids in school who were genuinely unique, which was shorthand for weird. On the other hand there were trendy kids who listened to whatever was brand new on the radio and dressed in the latest fashions. They stood out for trying so hard to fit in; they came off as mindlessly conformist and shallow. Perfect identity equilibrium, it seemed, lay somewhere between the extremes, between the oblivious weirdo and the shallow, self-absorbed trend watcher. I needed to figure out how to not quite blend in and not quite stand out.

The identity game only got more complicated when I left home for Bible college. I had hoped to finally "find myself" alongside all the intelligent men and women who had already found themselves, but what I got was the same paradoxical blend of "be yourself/fit in," only now it seemed that the stakes were higher. Now that we were away from home and out in the world, we were supposed to be grown-ups, but the increasing gravity of our decisions made us take ourselves even more seriously than we had as self-conscious high school kids. The people we hung out with, the conversations we engaged in, the clothes we wore—everything communicated something important about who we thought we really were. The books under our arm were like flashing signs announcing "cool," "conservative" or "dangerous" (Douglas Coupland, Josh McDowell, and Karl Barth, respectively.) A CD collection was about much more than taste; it spoke volumes about who you really were. The people who still liked heavy metal seemed stuck in the imagined glory days of high school. Hip hop fans were rebellious, dangerous, had probably used drugs at some point, and were definitely cooler than I could ever be. Snobs listened to classical music (conservative!) and jazz aficionados were intellectuals. Fans of "alternative music," which had exploded only a couple years prior, were open minded and non-conformist, but only if you happened to be into the various bands *before* they got big.

It was all part of the same game I had known my whole life but with a ramped-up, obsessive attention to detail, and identity still seemed depressingly arbitrary. My chosen groups of affiliation based on shared interests didn't seem to make me any more truly myself. Instead, I felt like I was learning to play roles, enact scripts, and abide by the unwritten rules of different groups. Seduced by a kind of selective conformity, I went along with something I pretended was my own, all the while playing the part someone else had given me.

At different times in our lives, most of us still get caught up in trying to figure how to be our true selves. Culture says that to be true to myself means to do whatever I feel like, as if doing so is somehow a sign of personal integrity. This includes an embrace—doing whatever I want—and a denial—cutting myself loose from all obligations, responsibilities, old-fashioned ideas, and traditions, anything that suggests submitting my will. The true self is anarchic, unfettered by what has been handed down. I must decide everything for myself, consider morality, responsibility, commitments, and relationships according to the standard that I discover or that I choose. Then I will be free; then I will be my self. Responsibilities and commitments to others are restrictive, inhibiting obligations that must not block my path toward self-actualization.

Though this might sound liberating, doing whatever I want is not necessarily being true to myself any more than making a commitment to someone is a betrayal of my true self. More than a century ago, G.K. Chesterton identified the madness of believing in oneself: "I know of men who believe in themselves more colossally than Napoleon or Caesar . . . The men [and women] who really believe in themselves are all in lunatic asylums . . . Believing utterly in oneself is a hysterical and superstitious belief."[1] I don't mean to challenge the virtue of integrity, or the goodness in pursuing a particular talent, or the need to resist cultural forces that want to turn us into a mindless herd, but when taken as a fundamental doctrine for how we ought to live, being true to oneself is tautological and isolating. To what self am I to be true if I don't know who I truly am? Am I defined by my actions? If I have done whatever I want to do, how do these experiences make me my true, and presumably unique, self? Am I myself because of the combination of places I've lived, people I've met, and things I've done? Am I the sum of my tastes and interests? Is that what makes me *me*? In this way, looking forever deeper inside myself for my true identity is like peeling the layers off an onion in search of the onion: in the end, there's nothing left.

Instead of simply looking within myself or adding up my tastes and experiences to find my true self, I find it much more fruitful to examine my identity through my relationships with others. In *The One, The Three and The Many*, Colin Gunton argues that we become ourselves through our relationships. "As made in the image of God," he writes, "we are closely bound up, for good or ill, with other human beings . . . [We] mutually constitute each other, make each other what [we] are."[2] Gunton argues that we are not just shaped by others—influenced by their tastes, ideas, teachings, or experiences—but that we

---

1. Chesterton, *Orthodoxy*, 6.

2. Gunton, *The One, The Three, and The Many*, 169.

actually *become* ourselves through our relationships. Obviously, the most primary and formative of my relationships is with my parents. Without my parents I literally would not exist. They made me, named me, loved me, and gave me language; they housed me, clothed me, fed me, raised me, and gave me siblings. There are, of course, countless other formative relationships from my childhood—with my siblings, cousins, aunts and uncles, camp counselors, piano teachers, neighbors, classmates, teachers—all of which have shaped me so indelibly that it's impossible to imagine myself apart from them. If Gunton is right, rather than thinking of others as a threat to my freedom and to my "true" self, I have become, and am still becoming, myself through my relationships with others. My relationships make up who—and whose—I am.

The doctrine of the independent, self-reliant individual forces us to view relationships with others as ultimately competitive, as though we are in a struggle against even those we love to define who we really are. I wholeheartedly agree that other people are a threat to our individualism—our wish to be self-determining, autonomous beings who only do what we choose. But this kind of "self" is no self at all. My self is not a finite resource of which I must be a cautious, stingy steward, but rather a gift I receive from others.

I see this most poignantly in my relationship with Erika. We started dating when we were just out of high school but then spent five years apart, and throughout those years, I ached to be with her, longed desperately for her, and wondered what she was doing and if she still thought of me. It sounds sentimental, I know, but I felt inescapably that part of me was missing. Once we were reunited and starting to plan for marriage, I realized that I needed her, that apart from her I was less myself. By loving and being loved I was taking a risk. I knew that my self was not my own. I'm sure that some would consider this a sign of a fragile psychological state or an unhealthy codependent relationship, but I think it indicates a truth: the two of us were becoming one. Today, as it was in Genesis, "it is not good for man (or woman) to be alone."

And the oneness of Erika and I in marriage is more than esoteric, disembodied spiritual abstraction. The two of us are one in very real, everyday ways; our love is particular and requires ongoing attention. She looks me in the eye and asks me how I'm doing because she can tell by my posture and my walk that something is bothering me, and when we talk I can tell whether or not she's really listening or distracted by her own concerns or worries by how long she holds my gaze.[3] She shares her own story and history—her temptations, fears, and life-long doubts, and those become part of who I am. We share a piece of toast with jam late in the evening, and we share a bed with one another. We share the stress of disciplining our young kids and the ongoing anxiety about how we're going to make ends meet. We share the blessings of our children, the jokes they try to tell, the way they dance to the *Where the Wild Things Are* soundtrack, their hugs that wrap around our thighs and almost pull us down. It's the oneness of love, the oneness of giving to one another. Oneness is spiritual and emotional, but it is certainly fleshy as well.

Everyday marriage asks me to give up the supposed right to be myself, yet under the vows of marriage, it is the place where I am most myself. It is not the sacrifice of martyrdom; it is the gift of love that gives graciously in return. I obey my vows, maintain the promise to be faithful to Erika, choose over and over again to enact the covenant of our wedding day witnessed by family, friends, and community. All of these run contrary to the myth of the truly independent individual, but this is what makes me *me*. The goal of marriage is not to come out on top; the goal is to love. The kinds of relationships prized by our culture—relationships that are supposed to enhance self-fulfillment, freely chosen "partnerships" that will increase self-actualization— depend on the assumption of the self-made individual, which is an illusion. No one can will themselves into being; all that we are and all that we have is gift.

The terror of infinite, limitless choice, dressed up as the freedom to choose from an endless array of relational possibilities, is radically

3. Offering wholehearted attention to one another is perhaps *the* greatest ongoing challenge of married life. One time when I was in grad school, I came home and found Erika in the kitchen, cleaning and organizing the kitchen, something I knew usually made her feel great. Just the two of us. At home. Alone. I had amorous thoughts and intentions.

I hugged Erika and kissed her neck, and took her by the hand and led her to the living room and onto the couch. After a minute or so of smooching, I could tell something wasn't quite right. I looked her in the eye, and in my best caring-and-connected husband voice asked her what was bothering her.

"I was thinking about whether or not we should try to use up the rest of that mozzarella in the fridge before it starts to get moldy."

different from maintaining a commitment "'till death separates us."
Whimsical relationships require none of the discipline, patience, trust
or forgiveness that a lifelong covenant demands. But in the end, one is
simply left with more choice, with the same, endless possibilities that
were there in the first place. A string of relationships adds to the list
of experiences, but never roots the self because these relationships are
always tenuous, requiring one to be on their guard in defense of their
increasingly elusive and fragile self.

My relationships place me. They say who and whose I am more
than any of the ways I might otherwise try to define myself. In marriage, my life is intimately woven together with Erika's. By my vows I
give up my "right" to my self. To live for and with my wife does not offer the exoticism of the possibility of going to bed with someone new
every night, but in the end I have found—or maybe been found by
—what I've been looking for: roots, belonging, meaning, acceptance,
healing, and love. Here, in the everydayness of love and the familiarity
of my vows is a satisfaction that runs deeper than the lightning-flash
promises of novelty and instant gratification that keep lonely lovers
jumping from one bed into the next, as if they may somehow stumble
over what they are looking for. Such "freedom" looks more like a kind
of insanity, doing the exact same thing over and over again in the exact
same way, each time imagining that the outcome will be new. Love
doesn't come more quickly by searching more frantically and desperately; you find it best when you slow down and stay in one place.

Jesus Loves

Your Penis,

Son

The first thing I remember about my penis was getting it caught in the zipper of my fuzzy, yellow pyjamas. My brother and sister and I had been staying with friends for a couple days while our parents took a little husband-wife getaway. Mom and Dad came to pick us up after supper, so we were all dressed in our PJ's and I remember getting ready to go, and for some reason I wasn't wearing any underwear (probably something embarrassing, i.e. I'd shat my last pair). The zipper on my one-piece pyjamas ran up from one knee right to the collar, and as I yanked up my zipper I caught the tip of my penis. It felt like a tiny dragon had clamped its jaws onto the tip of my teensy pecker. I then understood what they meant about zippers having "teeth." I don't remember any blood, but I do remember wailing. My sympathetic Dad carried me to the car.

Next thing I remember about my penis was an erection, surely not my first, but the first I remember because it was so uncomfortable. It was a summer evening and I couldn't sleep. Partly it was the heat and the lingering sunlight of summertime but mostly it was my erection that kept me awake. I usually slept on my stomach, but

28

every time I rolled over it felt like my penis had turned into a stick that kept poking into me. I'd roll onto my side and wait for it to go away, but every time I rolled back to my stomach to try to sleep it was still there. What to do?

"Dad," I called. He was in the family room sitting on the couch. "Dad?"

"Yes?" he said.

"Dad, I can't fall asleep because my penis is stiff."

If he laughed—surely he laughed, probably fell off the couch and ruptured something he laughed so hard—I didn't hear.

I didn't pay much attention to my penis again until the summer I turned eleven and my cousin Mitch told me that his brother Devon had learned to "shoot sperm." My cousins were missionaries in Pakistan and were back visiting for the summer. I had noticed that Devon's voice was a lot deeper than the rest of ours, and when we'd stop playing to go take a leak in the trees, I'd sometimes sneak a peak at his penis (I didn't yet know what "gay" meant, or worry about whether or not it applied to me) and I noticed that a) it seemed enormous, and b) he had hair down there. Mitch explained to me this had to do with shooting sperm. My cousin Dan and I camped out one night with Mitch, completely mystified as he explained the basics of shooting sperm.

"Here's how it works," he said. "You just think about a naked lady and then you rub your dick really, really fast. After a bit, you'll shoot sperm." It was the strangest thing I'd ever heard of. Did it come out like pellets or pop out like a tiny cork, or did the sperms come out one at a time? A few days later I tried rubbing my penis during a bath and tiny bits of dead skin came off. Was that the sperm? I didn't notice any sort of "shooting" action, but maybe "shooting" was just the word they used for it. Maybe the trouble was I hadn't been thinking about a naked lady. No luck there because I'd never seen one before. I dug a Sears catalog out of the closet and found the women's underwear section which had lots of pretty and nearly naked ladies, and tried it again, and POW! I don't remember shooting anything, but it sure felt good. So *this* is what he was talking about! I tried it again the next day: same thing. POW again! And just like that, I stumbled upon the big "M": masturbation.

A Christian adolescent boy's sex drive is sort of like learning to drive: it's exhilarating, out of control, and probably quite dangerous. Unlike driving a car, a sex drive is relentless. It doesn't let up, even if you want it to, no matter how much you pray or how diligently you try to channel all that hormonal energy into basketball or hockey or lacrosse or cricket or rowing or judo or jogging or running on the spot—something, *any*thing—to keep your mind off sex. Nobody ever told me "masturbation is a sin," but they did say, "lust is a sin," which automatically made masturbation a sin because it didn't go so well if all you did was think about holy, unsexy things.

That God gave me a raging libido and expected me to be good felt as fair as handing a pyromaniac a six-pack of Bic lighters and a ten-gallon barrel of diesel fuel and saying, "Now get out there and behave!" Maybe at some point there was an evolutionary advantage to boys maturing sexually in their early teens: young men, not yet strong enough to be warriors, were virile and eager, ready to help the tribe by reproducing. But nowadays, we live longer, marry later, and we're born into a culture that prizes lust as a virtue. Combine that with some religious morality and you end up with what I got: a fragmented, schizophrenic sense that sexuality is the best thing I could imagine and something very, very dirty.

All of this is fresh for me now because I have a little boy of my own. At four months old he discovered his penis and he would yank on it and stretch it so hard I would cringe and wince, but he would giggle so hard he'd nearly fall off the change table. When he was two, he fussed and fought at diaper time, but once his diaper was off, he'd grab his penis and say "Touch penis? Touch penis?" as he'd pull, twist, spin, bend, and pinch his little male member. "Yes, you can touch your penis," I'd tell him, thinking, *Just you wait, buddy. You have no idea how much fun you're going to have with that thing one day.*

But what'll it be: guilt or fun? Will he suffer through the sexual angst of his teenage years feeling like his penis is a curse, or will he believe, deep down, that sexuality is fundamentally good? Will he beg God to help him stop masturbating, or will he live with it and enjoy it without attaching eternal consequences to his pleasure? How will I talk to my boy about the *gravitas* and consequences of sex without unnecessarily poisoning the gift of his sexuality with shovelfuls of shame? When the time comes for me to talk to him about sex, can I help him to see that sex is more than a pleasurable slapping together of naked bodies, something to do on a Friday night? I'm getting ahead of myself, I know—he's just barely potty trained—but even now I wonder if I will be able to help him understand that a penis is not just for peeing but for having a good time, but that that good time is loaded with meaning, responsibility, relationship, covenant, and most of all, love. Much of the tangible existential whallop of sex has been softened by condoms and birth control pills. It used to be that a roll in the sack led to a baby. Nowadays we imagine we have made sex "safe" because we can go at it without much risk of babies or diseases. But does any thinking man or woman truly believe that a tiny sheath of rubber can make sex safe? It's as safe as putting a dog-leash on a full-grown lion. A condom might keep two people from making a baby or from catching some exotic sounding, painful, pubic disease, but it does not make sex safe.

My parents taught me that sex was a beautiful thing, but only in its proper place, which is in marriage, and I used to blame them for all the guilt and fear and shame I felt, and still feel, about being sexual. Even now, I still wrestle with the deep-down feeling that sex is somehow fundamentally dirty. (I don't blame my parents anymore because I have no doubts whatsoever that they did their very best to raise me well. I've become much more accepting of whatever shortcomings or mistakes my parents might have made now that I'm a dad myself. Here's my five-word summary of parenthood: helluvalot harder than it looks.)

I want to make sure my son knows about goodness before he knows about sin. I don't want him to think his body is a mistake, or that his desires are dirty and make him a bad person. I want him to know that whatever other moral issues it might involve, masturbation is undeniably pleasurable, and that pleasure in the grand scheme of things is entirely God's idea.

So son, if you want to play with your penis, go for it. When one day those hormones in your body kick into high gear and all you seem to be able to think about is sex and you discover just how much fun masturbation can be, don't let guilt and shame take the fun out of it for you. If the kids at school try to tell you it will make you go blind or make you crazy, you can always look to your dad for proof that they're lying. And if well-meaning religious folks tell you it's an abomination or that God is scowling at you every time you touch yourself, remember this: God made your penis. Your penis was his idea in the first place and if it's true that Jesus loves you, if there's any truth to that at all, then you can believe with all your heart that Jesus loves your penis, too.

How I Discovered that Sex Is Not Nearly as Dirty as I Used to Think It Was

My dad gave me my first and pretty much only sex talk when I was five years old. After supper one night, Dad said he needed drive to Hanna to pick up some parts for the tractor and he wondered if I wanted to come along. Going for an evening drive with Dad sounded like fun, especially since it meant that we were going to be out past my bedtime. But there was more on the agenda that night than just a fun drive with Dad. Like a lot of dads with kids my age, he was anxious to explain the basics of sex to me before some kid at school offered their own snickering, exaggerated, and confused version of where babies come from. We weren't far into our hour-long round trip when he started into a rehearsed explanation about the differences between boys and girls and the facts about babies and so on. I was too young to pick up on the important details, too young to make any sense of the explanations, definitely too young to have any genuine interest, so I made up a little game of my own and counted the old telegraph poles beside the railroad tracks that ran next to the highway.

33

Three significant details stuck with me. The first was that there were more telegraph poles than I could count; second, I now knew that Mary, the mother of Jesus, was a "virgin," though I missed the explanation of what exactly a virgin was; third, I learned that some day when I grew up I would have a wet dream. I missed the explanation about that too, because I ended up thinking it had something to do with the way I drooled on my pillow in my sleep.

My real sex education started in school, informally and graphically thanks to a huge kid named Gary from the grade ahead. His repertoire of dirty jokes was positively astounding and he knew the actual meaning of all the swear words I had ever heard. I was sure his knowledge about sex was encyclopedic. I gradually picked up the basic information about sex—the different names for the different parts, which of those parts went where, the required motions, sounds, and banter, and the results that were to be expected. Though I didn't understand most of his jokes, I laughed anyway (for which I felt very guilty), but everything I learned was entirely abstract. Sex sounded fascinating and completely bizarre, but I honestly had my doubts about whether it was even real or just something Gary had made up. I had never seen anything pornographic, had never even seen a picture of a naked woman.

Thanks to a fairly straightforward explanation from an older cousin, I discovered masturbation before I ever had a wet dream. Puberty and the hormones hit like a tornado that struck without any warning, and I was smack-dab in the middle of something I wasn't expecting and didn't ask for, with no real sense of how to weather the storm. My interest in sex suddenly went from abstract curiosity and childish fascination with dirty jokes to wild, non-stop, testosterone-induced obsession. Although I had always liked girls (I don't remember ever thinking of them as the least bit "yucky") my interest in the girls in my grade and the girls in my sister's grade, as well as pretty much all the girls on TV, the middle-aged woman who cut my hair, the short, young woman who worked the till at the grocery store, the teller at the bank with dyed red hair and fancy makeup, my much older second cousin's beautiful girlfriend that I saw only once a year— let's just say girls and women everywhere—suddenly went from innocent, pleasant enjoyment to overpowering, irresistible, frightening attraction. There was nothing resembling pornography in our house, and I never once even flipped through a *Playboy* magazine until I was twenty, simply out of the paralyzing fear of getting caught by someone I knew. But for years I pored over the tantalizing lingerie section of the Sears catalog, entranced and absolutely fascinated by women and their curvy, otherworldly beauty. But my patchwork sex education left me with some basic unanswered questions and a powerful overall impression that whatever appeal it might hold, sex was ultimately dirty, unwholesome and sinful.

My strongest and most lasting impressions about sex have probably come from television, which was, for the first half of my life, my primary source of pop culture consumption. Having now lived almost entirely without television for the last seventeen years, I'm starting to understand more clearly how thoroughly television educated me, and I've come to think that whatever good television might have to offer is entirely outweighed by the damage it does, especially in regards to sex.[1] Never one to mince words, Wendell Berry calls television, "the greatest disrespecter and exploiter of sexuality that the world has ever seen," which is used to "pimp for the exceedingly profitable 'sexual revolution.'"[2] I can't point to a single episode of a particular sitcom or drama, nor a particular brand or ad campaign that created such a strong impression of what sexuality ought to be, but the cumulative effect of the countless sexually charged televised images inscribed me with a sexual mythology that I am, to this day, trying to *un*learn.

The television-based mythology of sex asks me to hold two fundamentally incompatible assumptions simultaneously. The first is that sex is the ultimate human experience, that beneath every interaction between two adult human beings lies an overt, fundamental, unavoidable, and entirely desirable sexual energy. The freedom to have (consensual) sex with anyone you want is almost considered a basic right.

1. If you're reading this and thinking, "Oh great, here he goes again, ripping into television," I hope you won't take it personally, especially if you consider yourself a fan of the medium. But I won't back down. Yes, here I go. I'm picking on television yet again because I see it as the 24-7 summons of the belltower, calling us to worship at the cathedrals of Mammon—the Shopping Mall and the Big Box Retailer. I think it celebrates every one of the seven deadly sins as virtuous, and so I consider it my duty to speak ill of it whenever I have the chance. I don't know if that justifies the rant, but there's my explanation.

2. Berry, "Sex, Economy, Freedom, and Community," 124.

Even marriage no longer offers any real boundary for sex; in general, any sort of commitment in a relationship can be considered short-term. First-date sex is a good idea, considering that so-called "sexual compatibility" can make or break a relationship, and men and women should strive to be the best possible lover, sort of like being the best worker in the office, or the best performer on the swim team, because a strong, dynamic, free and open sexuality is central to one's identity.

Nearly everything in consumer culture—from cars to cosmetics, soft drinks to software, cell phones to cleaning products—is marketed by making some sort of implicit or explicit promise about sex, reinforcing the sex-as-the-ultimate-experience myth. A wide range of books offers new, comprehensive techniques and updated versions of ancient sexual practices to turn the reader's presumably boring, day-to-day sex life into a carnival of thrilling, mind-blowing, orgasmic adventures. (On a cursory browse through the "Sexuality" section at the local bookstore, I saw *Cosmic Coupling*, *365 Nights of Passion*, and perhaps most promising, at least for someone with my religious background, *The Sex Bible*). New books promise to reveal secret, newly discovered, and exotic, multicultural means of achieving the most satisfying orgasms. (Same cursory browse: *The Orgasm Answer Book*, *The Multi Orgasmic Couple*, and the book that no doubt tops them all, *The Everything Orgasm Book*). Adult novelty stores offer an overwhelming range of lubes and lotions, sex toys, books, and movies, to make sex more satisfying. Of course, all of these things—sexy cars, sexy eye shadow, sexy books or sexy toys—carry a price tag. Judging by what these things promise, it's clear that the best things in life certainly are *not* free. But now that we have thoroughly separated sex from primitive and cumbersome things like procreation or marriage, we can—and should—be doing it more and more and more. Abstinence and chastity are indications that one suffers from psychological issues of some kind—repression or denial—or is trapped by a narrow-minded, fundamentalist-tinged moral prudishness that is hopelessly outdated and out of touch with reality.

At the same time, the television-based mythology asks us to believe that sex is nothing really significant, no more than a fun (but ultimately meaningless) slapping together of naked bodies. As the gorgeous men and women of Hollywood shuffle from one bed to another, on-screen and off, they wittingly or unwittingly teach an informal sex-ed curriculum that completely trivializes sexuality. Sex comes off looking like a harmless pastime with no greater moral or spiritual significance than video games, shopping, or recreational swimming. Sex is not even an intimate exchange of bodily fluids, for that would not be considered "safe." Beyond individual consent, there are no prerequisite promises prior to sex, nor should sex with another person imply any sort of lasting promise. Sex is an easy and natural coupling, a simple equation: one plus one (both of whom must have properly functioning pleasure parts) equals all you need for a good time. Crassly speaking, the primary measure of an individual's healthy sexuality is a varied and lengthy list of sexual conquests. Sex is simple and perfectly healthy, the sort of thing we should expect from just about everyone and anyone.

We are told, in other words, that sex is everything, and sex is nothing.

It sounds very appealing—at least to me—that these contradictory things could be true at the same time. The idea that I could have as much sex as I wanted, wherever and whenever the urge happened to strike, with no lasting consequences is the stuff of wild sexual fantasy. But the *reality* of everything/nothing sex is, without exception, disastrous. "Unlimited sex with zero consequence" is the fundamental philosophy of the pornography industry and the obscenely profitable, make-believe sexual fantasy world. The real-life damage inflicted by pornography runs top to bottom, from the habits and secrets of the casual viewer of free internet porn to the highest paid, highly exploited, thoroughly objectified actress, and everyone in between. The reality of everything/nothing sex brings to mind a man I know who, by all appearances, was a work-a-day, church-going, monthly-tithing family man. But over the span of more than thirty years, he spent hundreds of thousands of dollars on visits with prostitutes, escorts, and trips to massage parlors without his wife or his kids or his friends having any idea what he was doing. He acted as though sex was everything, that he couldn't possibly get enough of it with the woman he had married, and was therefore willing to risk his job, family, grandkids, and community to get some; and at the same time, he pretended it was nothing, like a private hobby that didn't need to interfere with daily domestic responsibilities or work or church commitments. It took more than three decades, but eventually his secret sex-as-everything/

nothing double life caught up with him, and he lost everything. (I don't consider his story grounds for gloating about my moral superiority. Far from it. Because I, too, am a male and have an appetite for lust that shocks me, and because I locate my sexual temptations and sins on the same continuum as this man's philandering, it scares the hell out of me.)

What makes television so infuriating is the very thing that makes it so intoxicating: it is almost irresistibly attractive, which makes it mesmerizingly good at convincing us to buy things. The advertisers have seduced us into believing that we can buy something that will satisfy our deepest longings for a healthy body, a loving relationship, satisfying sex, or a sense of meaning, significance, and purpose. The fundamental lie in all of this, of course, is not that things like love and sexual satisfaction are good, but that they are easy, and that you can get them by buying something.

But the most compelling and enticing advertisements are absolutely disingenuous because the advertisers hawking their wares fundamentally depend on our continued *dis*satisfaction. If advertising was truly about sharing information about the different sorts of products that are available (which is exactly what I recently heard one prominent Canadian ad-writer claim he's doing) ads would include statements like: "when used properly, this shampoo can clean your hair and leave it with a lasting, overpowering, artificial, floral scent, and is guaranteed to have no part in making you irresistibly attractive to the opposite sex or making you look like a movie star;" or "beer is an alcoholic beverage that cannot in any way remedy loneliness in any lasting fashion, but can cause intoxication and thereby impair the consumer's better judgment when trying to understand verbal or nonverbal cues from the opposite sex;" or "this automobile is an expensive, dangerous, noisy, gas-guzzling, stinky machine that cannot possibly improve the quality of your sex-life and will ultimately break down, rust, crash, malfunction or otherwise disintegrate, but in the meantime, if used properly and carefully, is useful for rapid ground-level transportation."

We're so intensely bombarded with media and advertising imagery that the boundary between real, everyday life and the ad-driven, make-believe world of digital retouches and professional actors relying on expensive age-defying surgeries is becoming increasingly difficult to discern. We want to dress like, talk like, act like, think like, kiss like, and make love like the people on TV. The images shape us, and we start to think of our relationships as though they were products, just like everything else, satisfying or dissatisfying, depending on how closely they resemble the relationships on the sitcoms or in the advertisements. We tell television jokes as though they were our own and discuss television relationships as though they were real. We start thinking that sex should be like it is on television, and if it isn't, we're in need of some new technique or toy, or maybe it's time to find ourselves another lover with whom we can be more sexually compatible. We line up to buy the products, re-making ourselves in the image of the elusive and unreal fabrications of the advertisers. We may want our lives to be like theirs, but our real lives never match up to the supposed ideal, and we end up buying more and more stuff, foolishly believing that this time will be different.

Now that I've spent a whole bunch of pages complaining about how television and consumer culture have got sex all wrong, it's high time for me to start saying some good things about sex, but I realize that so far I've been stalling. It is easier and safer for me to talk about what sex *isn't*, but as far as what sex *is*, I'm tempted to end with a footnote pointing everyone to Mike Mason's chapter on sex in *The Mystery of Marriage,* or the title chapter in Wendell Berry's *Sex, Economy, Freedom and Community*, or Lauren Winner's *Real Sex.*

I'm stalling, not because I'm completely ignorant about sex— I've been married for ten years and I have two kids—but because I've got some sexual hang-ups. My hang-ups are, in some ways, secondary I suppose, because before I have issues about sex, I have issues about my body. Mostly I am ashamed of my body, of being a body, ashamed of other people's bodies, and not just the parts that obviously have something to do with sex. Like the majority of descendants of Enlightenment philosophy, I'm more used to considering myself a *thinking* being rather than a *physical* being, a mind rather than a body. More often than not I live with the attitude that my body is a burden. I worry about lower back pain (just typing that made me sit up a bit straighter) and I know I don't eat enough fresh fruit and vegetables (I'd rather have a couple slices of toast with lots of butter and a deep layer of homemade jam, or maybe my snack standby of Cokeandchips) and I always feel guilty about that. Sometimes I have a bit of dandruff that, thankfully, seems to just sort of go away on its own, because I don't know how I got it or how to treat it. From time to time I have a scruffy beard, often for the simple fact that I can't be bothered to shave on a regular basis. I recently started jogging because I've begun worrying that I don't get enough cardiovascular exercise. I'm ashamed that I crave sweets and like to buy chewy candy, and I'm conscious that I have a socially acceptable addiction to coffee. After I take a bath and I'm standing in front of the mirror, I look at my arms and think, I wish my muscles looked more like Brad Pitt's muscles in *Legends of the Fall*, but the fact is my arms look pretty scrawny, more John Turturro than Pitt. Even now when I hold my kids for very long, my arms start to ache and I sometimes ask myself, Could it be that I'm not strong enough to be a good dad?

Whether our bodies have parts that are too big or too small, parts too flat or too round, parts that don't seem to work as well as we want them to, or not at all or parts that are missing, earhair, nosehair, or backhair where we don't want it and comb-overs to cover the wide open cranial vistas where the hair used to be, uninviting odours, pimples, wrinkles, corns, or calluses, everyone's body has plenty to be embarrassed about. And if that's true, we should all breathe a collective sigh of relief and let ourselves go a bit—let the eyebrows get bushy or skip showering for a week—because we're universally embarrassing. But even though the most personal things are sometimes the most universal, it doesn't necessarily make them any easier to handle. All my life, I've watched some of the most beautiful people I know spend so much time and effort changing their bodies with such an array of chemicals, diets, vicious exercise programs, processes, and procedures it looks like they are at war with themselves.

Before our bodies are anything else, before they are awkward or pimply or balding sources of shame, they are gifts from a gracious God, and all the nasty feelings we can come up with to denigrate our own bodies can never undo that primary, fundamental mystery, that ontological truth about who we are: bearers of the image of God. And when we start from there, I think we can all find some room to celebrate our bodies and to be grateful.

I'm stalling, too, because for all the public spectacle our culture makes of sexuality, real sex is so deeply personal and profoundly intimate that only the two lovers wrapped up, in and around each other can ever really know what it's about. The reality of loving, faithful sex is almost too mysterious and holy to look at. The advertisers (as well as the pornographers) understand very well the raw appeal of sexuality and the basic mechanics of sex, but they have no clue about *love*, without which sex is as meaningless as a fart. Love is to sex what gardening, cooking, taste, smell, nutrition, and care is to food. Sex without love is like a flavorless food-pill that that can be swallowed with a drink of water. It promises to provide the sustenance and nutrition of an old-fashioned meal without any of the hassle of choosing what to make, selecting the ingredients, preparing and eating the meal, and cleaning up. It is a cheap substitute, a commodity like anything else. It can get the basic job done, but the rich, satisfying, meaning-filled pleasures of it all are nowhere to be found. But, then, talking honestly and clearly about something as profoundly real as sex is infinitely more difficult than plucking sex entirely out of context, isolating it from the relationship between two people and their kids and the community that supports them and their vows, and splaying titillating images on a billboard or a television screen to try to sell perfume and shoes.

More than anything else, I struggle to write about the good side of sex because my sense of sexuality is woven together with shame. My earliest memories of sexual feelings were an intense combination of excitement and shame, leaving me with the impression that sex was dirty and degrading—at least in part because the strict moral teaching I grew up with was in such stark contrast with my informal, school-playground sex education. I don't blame my parents or my church or that kid Gary and his dirty jokes or anyone else. I wasn't sexually abused as a child or exposed to pornography at an early age. No one ever told me sex was shameful, but my gut-sense of shame is strong. And despite my best intentions and efforts to change my heart and mind, the shame hasn't gone away. Ten years of marriage has mined the top layers off my shame and revealed a lot more underneath, and I trust that the love that has healed me so far will continue to put my heart, body, and soul back together. Even if I am never quite whole, even if my sexuality is always broken, love keeps pulling me towards the light, helping me heal a little bit at a time.

To combat the consumerist myths of love and sexuality, and to address my own deep, ongoing struggle to find a healthy sense of sexuality, the Christian myth that describes where we've come from, what we are, and where we are going offers a radical alternative. Now I realize it is unpopular and decidedly countercultural to look to Christianity for a meaningful antidote to our deeply confused ideas about sexuality. Every pop-culture portrayal I can think of depicts the church as a thoughtless, prudish, moralistic, repressive, authoritarian, squeamish killjoy, thoroughly uncomfortable with any honest discussion of sex. Pop culture says the church is anti-sex, full of warnings about the profound spiritual risks and dangers of sex, treating it like it's a problem we don't have to talk about in any meaningful or graphic way so long as we can pretend (and convince enough followers) that deep down it is very, very bad. I'm not all that interested in trying to defend the church's historical record on sexuality, though I'm not sure that non-church culture has done a more admirable job with sex. But Christianity itself is ultimately, inescapably *fleshy*—that's precisely the point of the Incarnation—and perhaps the goodness of sexuality has survived the general reluctance and squeamishness of the church because despite the perpetual debasement it has suffered, sex is ultimately God's idea, and because authentic Christian spirituality is as fleshy as sex itself.

Any critic who derides Christianity for being anti-sex should have a good close look at Genesis 2, the story of Adam and Eve, where the man and woman are brought together for the first time. In the first creation account, God says to the man and woman, "Be fruitful and increase in number," though, let's be honest, it's unlikely the two of them—surprised to be seeing one another for the very first time, naked, and not feeling any shame—would have needed any real encouragement to do what was no doubt the very first thing on their minds. Sex is an original part of God's perfect creation. Human history has unfolded "east of Eden," where we are constantly jostled and misled by the sin that drives a wedge in our relationships with one another and with God, and human sexuality, along with everything else in creation, has suffered from the damage of sin. But as Mike Mason writes in his brilliant, insightful book, *The Mystery of Marriage*:

> [T]hough banished from Eden, the first couple were not banished from one another's arms, nor from the marriage bed.

This is one garden to which God continues to welcome husbands and wives, and where they are privileged to return again and again in order to expose their nakedness and be healed of secrecy and separateness.[3]

Whether or not Adam and Eve were literally the two first human beings on the planet is not the point of the story; the point is that the untameable, passionate, exhilarating erotic energy that makes us wild for one another now is the same untameable, passionate, exhilarating erotic energy that's been there from the very beginning. We were truly made for one another. Sex has been central to God's idea of humankind from the very beginning.

The central Old Testament theme of the covenantal blessing of Israel is entirely dependent upon sex and procreation. Beginning with Abraham and Sarah, God promises a nation as numerous as the stars, though the two of them were childless at the time. Abraham was ninety-nine, Sarah nintey when God reminded them of his promised blessing, and Genesis 17 says that Abraham's response was to fall down and laugh (maybe he laughed so hard he fell over). Though it sounds as unlikely to us as it did to the two of them, Abraham and Sarah made a baby the old-fashioned way. It's absurd to try to read the bible as anti-sex or even a-sexual because the very same man/woman baby-making process that produced Isaac and Ishmael and the entire Jewish race is the same baby-making process of today. Sex isn't incidental to blessing; it's central.

Jump to Song of Solomon, which the playwright Lucia Frangione calls, "a slender bit of guilt-free erotica that somehow slipped into the holy scriptures and stayed."[4] Christians have long struggled with the overtly erotic tone of the book, at times treating it as an allegory of God's love to try to dodge the graphic, libidinous, inescapably sexual language of the poem. Allegory or not, there's no escaping the fact that Song of Solomon is raunchy. It seems to me that if it is, in fact, an allegory, that simply makes the overt sexuality of it all the more compelling and celebratory because if raunchy sex is the metaphor God uses to describe his relationship to his people, only lovers who've feasted on one another's naked bodies will really make any sense of what he's talking about.

3. Mason, *The Mystery of Marriage*, 118.

4. Frangione, *Espresso*, 58.

The most compelling evidence that Christianity is seriously pro-sex is the Incarnation, the heart of Christian faith. Orthodox Christian doctrine has stood firm in the belief that Jesus was no part-human or pseudo-human: he was *all* human, just as he was all God. That, to me, is the ultimate, absolute mark of validity of my own body, that the creator of the universe[5] took on flesh just like mine. His birth would have been a lot like when my son was born: visceral, excruciating, shockingly messy, and profoundly miraculous. Mary would have nursed him at her breast, and just like every other little baby, sweet little baby Jesus probably crapped a diaperful at least a thousand times before he was finally potty trained. Surely there were times he literally would have been a snot-nosed kid. I'm sure he picked his nose. I've never met a kid yet who didn't.

I've got a picture in my head of Jesus as a placid child, a stoic look on his face, engaged in profound and perfectly dry spiritual dialogue with his local rabbi, but I'm sure a more realistic picture is Jesus howling over his scraped knee which he got while racing around the neighborhood with the other kids, and yelping when he gouged a chunk out of his palm with a chisel when he was in the woodshop with Joseph. Playing with other kids or working in the carpentry shop, Jesus would have had to stop now and then to take a leak. Like everyone who's ever lived, Jesus' stomach would have growled before supper, and he probably enjoyed a satisfying belch at the end of a meal of fish soup, bread, and wine. At the end of a hard day's work in the great heat of midsummer, I'll bet he smelled as strongly as I do at the end of a day hauling bricks and mortar up four flights of scaffold. I bet that when he was out walking with the disciples he liked to kick stones just for fun, discovering that split-second moment when he'd line up the stone to aim for and his brain and body made the subtle adjustments to his pace and step to get the footwork just-so to kick the stone he'd been aiming for.[6] Just like you, Jesus would have loved the taste of a cool

5. I don't believe in a literal six-day creation, or that the earth is 6,000 years old, but I do believe that God is behind the whole thing, that he made it, sustains it, and loves it, and that God's active love is ultimately what still holds the whole thing together.

6. If you're not into fishing and you don't work at a coffee shop where you can experience simple little tricks with paper coffee cups or the art of creating a perfect espresso, kicking a stone is another satisfying small wonder—a miracle of bodiliness—that can dazzle you if you pay close attention to the cues, sensations,

drink of water in the middle of a hot day. And although the Bible is mum about it, Jesus would have experienced puberty, wild surges of testosterone, and a sex drive just like the rest of us.

It almost sounds blasphemous to talk about Jesus taking a leak or having a libido, but this is undeniably orthodox Christian belief. We usually don't talk about it, probably because it seems unspiritual, but maybe it would help us be more at home in our own bodies if we did. Even though statements about Jesus' body and its functions seem crass, it's impossible to outdo the fundamental crassness of Jesus' crucifixion. We can speak without shame about the ordinary things of Jesus' daily living because his extraordinarily violent, bloody, human death, his *bodily* death, is central to everything the church has to say about who he is. Jesus' aphoristic wisdom and miracles and spiritual teaching are impossible to separate from his bodiliness, and following him makes it impossible for us to escape our own fleshiness. The doctrine of the Incarnation rightly gets in the way of the church's misguided attempts to find easy, dismissive answers about crass, bodily things like sex. Everything about our bodies is lifted up in Jesus.

Now, after all that, here are the only three things I really know about sex: sex is about love, sex is about pleasure, and sex is about babies.

But that's no way to end a whole chapter on sex, so I'll add this:

Sex is mostly a mystery to me. It takes more practice than I would have thought, and the attention and discipline it requires now is a lot more work than it was for us on the honeymoon.

Sex is a carefully cultivated sense of wonder at the miracles of skin and hair and muscle. It teaches patience, learning about who your lover really is, and it teaches humility, letting your lover know who you are. It's about trust, awe and wonder at this mysterious other.

Sex is a trick to get otherwise thoughtful, rational people into marriage and into bed and to get them procreating, but it's a damn good trick and I'm certainly willing to go along with it.

Sex is passionate, and sex is playful. It's exceptionally beautiful, sweaty, cumbersome, imperfect, awkward, and above all, fleshy (thank God!).

---

and adjustments as feet, hands, and torso all take their cues from the brain which gets it's information from your body's nerves, your eyes, and your inner ear—at least it's fascinating to me.

Sex is physical, spiritual, and emotional.

Sex breaks my heart and it heals my soul.

Sometimes sex is everyday and routine and unspectacular; sometimes it is surprising, spontaneous, unexpected, novel, brilliant.

Sex is like nothing I could have imagined, and is more than I could have hoped for.

And that, I believe, is just the beginning.

A Single Footnote

to a

Big Idea

CHAPTER 7

If you are able, have children.*

* I used to think marriage was hard. Then we had kids.

Kids change everything, and when I say change I mean "make unbelievably more difficult." They laugh at, scream at, and ignore your most noble plans—everything from what you were hoping to do later tonight to what you had in mind for the next twenty years—create levels of exhaustion you never would have imagined your body could tolerate, unapologetically humble you by revealing stores of nasty emotions you maybe never knew were there, and they make everything more complicated, and by everything I mean *everything*—from making supper tonight to making plans to visit friends next winter to making love to making ends meet and pretty much everything in between. And yet, I say it again: if you are able, have children. Which is perhaps even more bold than getting married because by the time you actually meet your child for the first time, when that wiggling, fussing, pooping, helpless, utterly dependent, loaf-of-bread-sized person enters the world, you've tied yourself in "'till death do us part" once again, only this time it's like an arranged marriage because you have no idea who this person is or what they're like, only that they're yours to love, raise, feed, clean up and clean up after, protect, teach, train, discipline, and otherwise care for.

If you don't already have a child or two or six, talking like this is, I imagine, less likely to convince you that it really is, in fact, a good idea to have kids and more likely to convince you to run to the nearest pharmacy and stock up on condoms or book the next available appointment at the vasectomy clinic, but I still truly believe that, even though it will most likely turn out to be among the Top Five hardest things you've ever done (probably #1), if you are able, have children.

I don't want to sentimentalize children or parenthood. It's positively shocking how one tiny little person can make even the most basic everyday tasks so difficult. Becoming a parent to a newborn is like living in a snowglobe that God tips on its side, shakes, and spins while he flicks the lights on and off and turns the radio to a not-quite-tuned-in station with the volume up to nine, finally setting the snowglobe back on the mantle to see what happens next. For a full year after Molly was born, I honestly felt like I was walking a very thin line that bordered on insanity. I'm prone to depression to begin with—I come from a long line of melancholy Danes on my mom's side and a handful of brooding, introverted Scots from my dad's—so it wasn't a complete surprise that the transition to being a father was seriously disorienting. But knowing it might be difficult didn't make the transition any easier. Becoming a dad felt like it came with a mountain of expectations I had no idea how to fulfill. Molly was born at home, a planned homebirth assisted by midwives, and our very first trip as a new family was less than two hours later to the hospital. We borrowed a car and carseat and drove downtown to St. Paul's Hospital. I dropped Erika off at the front door (Q. You dropped her off? A. Yes. Q. You dropped off the mother of your child *two hours after she gave birth*? A. Yes. Q. For heaven's sake, what in the world were you thinking? A. I wasn't.) and drove about three blocks until I finally found a parking space. I carried Molly in her carseat, switching her back and forth between my left and right hand, and every time my arms started to ache and I had to switch hands, I honestly wondered: Am I strong enough to be a dad? That was the first in a very, very long line of insecurities I've faced as a dad, and I have not yet reached the end. I feel unqualified for this. I know that I don't know what I'm doing.

But.

But I would not un-wish my kids for anything I could ask or imagine. As I write, I can hear my two young kids, Molly (age six) and Jackson (age three) playing downstairs, alternating back and forth between generous, cooperative, harmonious, imaginative play and full-throated, red-in-the-face screaming that's likely to end up with one of them hitting the other with whatever's handy if either Erika or I doesn't step in soon. Trying to be gentle with Molly when we're in the church basement after the service and putting on our layers of winter clothes to go home and she's being pouty, grumpy, disobedient, and defiant in front of all the other families whose kids are being polite and gentle and perfectly obedient, or patient with Jack when he's in his seat at the table and decides to have an "I DON'T LIKE THAT IT'S YUCKY" moment when guests are over and we're all sitting down to the supper I've just spent three hours working on makes me realize that Erika and I had no real idea whatsoever about what we were getting ourselves into when we decided to have kids (and when I'm feeling particularly discouraged and cynical, wondering if there's some possible way we can now get out).

Like the big bad fight between Erika and I that never really goes away, sometimes I look at my kids and think, I didn't ask for this. For the love of all things good, where did these two little creatures come from? I know, I know, a couple of passionate (and not unplanned) rolls in the hay and VOILA! We're parents! We chose this; we planned it. But why didn't anyone tell us what it would really be like? Seriously, there ought to be rules for this sort of thing. Kids ought to come equipped with flashing red lights and big yellow warning labels, and parenthood should require numerous university degrees and the signing of lengthy and detailed waivers.

Yet there are moments of such pure beauty and wonder as a father. At times, the simple presence of one of my children is so truly awesome that I feel like I might evaporate. The moment Molly was born was the moment I first believed that human beings are holy creatures. (At what point do we lose that sense of awe? How do our children go from wonderful to frustrating? When do we stop staring in amazement at newborns and learn how to see others as a threat? How do we create enemies?) My kids can say and do things so adorable and lovely I want to freeze them in time, never let them grow out of their beautiful innocence, sweetness, and wonder, always keep them little. They are as much a part of me as breathing.

It's a curious thing to have kids in our scientific/technological age, where we assume ever-increasing levels of mastery and control over every aspect of our lives. Because we're used to order and planning and independence and privacy and control, and because we've made it so incredibly easy *not* to have babies, I feel like I need some solid, rational justification for having them. It used to be that sex led to babies. Now we have condoms (his or hers), spermicidal foams, plugs and caps, once-a-day pills or once-a-year injections, scientifically accurate fertility awareness techniques, and low-invasive, below-the-belt, child-preventative day-surgeries (his or hers) that have made sex so babyless we could theoretically have infinite amounts of sex with zero babies. Add to this un-baby state of sex the gloomy statistics about global overpopulation, the ecological footprint of the average North American child, and the endless ways that kids complicate career plans, free time, and love life, and sometimes it's tough to come up with any rational reasons *to* have children. I've said to my children before, "You're so cute I want to eat you," which always elicits a giggle and a "No, Dad!" But a lot of the time my kids aren't so sweet. They're more like vegetables: I really don't want to eat them, but I know they're supposed to be good for me. And I'm not always entirely sure why we had them.

Thankfully, not everything comes down to a rational decision. For all the thinking and planning that went into it, in the end, we had kids for the same reason we got married: we wanted to. As with marriage, we really didn't know what we were getting ourselves into. We are a well-intentioned mom and dad, Erika and I, but we're in way over our heads, fumbling along, at times feeling like this parenting thing is really a cinch, and at other times feeling hopelessly, desperately lost. Both of us have discovered deep wells of anger and impatience we didn't know were there. Parenting is harder than either of us ever would have imagined, but even so, it is a good thing. I trust that it's good in ways that I can't always see and don't always understand.

Marriage already taught me that what is easy isn't necessarily what's best; parenthood has turned that into a lifestyle.

I don't see my friends as much as I used to now, don't go to concerts more than about once a year, and I spend a lot less time in the music store and a lot more time in the kids' books section of the library. I'm usually in bed by 10:30, up by 5:30 making coffee and grabbing a few hours of quiet before the kids get revved up and start requiring my attention. I'm sure I must have changed more than a thousand poopy diapers, and I've even done the very same heroic "catch your kid's puke in your own hands" maneuver that my Mom did so many *ha!* times, and I did it without gagging. I've started eating more raw vegetables because I want to set a good example for my kids, and I quit smoking, mostly for my kids too. I can eat my kids leftovers, even the pieces they've chewed on a few times then spit out. My stupid magic tricks leave my kids breathless, and my fairly unimpressive physical strength is substantially greater than theirs, enough to make me seem like a superhero in their eyes: if they're suddenly so tired they can't even walk, I can carry one on my shoulders and one in my arms.

I think that if Erika and I had not had kids and the two of us had simply had one another to gaze at for the rest of our lives, our love could have only grown so far. We're side-by-side rather than face-to-face more often than not now, but I trust that this journey of parenthood is taking us to the same kinds of good places marriage has. Learning to love Erika was good preparation for loving my kids; learning to love them helps make me the person I want to be.

So just to be sure that I'm making the point I set out to make and not mistakenly steering you in some other direction, I'll mention it one more time, and then I won't bring it up again: if you are able, have children.

Covenantal Love

The Means
and the End
Is Love

CHAPTER 8

Progress and love have nothing in common
Jesus healed a blind man's eyes with mud.

—Peter Case,
"Poor Old Tom," from the album,
The Man With the Blue Postmodern Fragmented Neo-
Traditionalist Guitar

For a full year after Erika and I were married, I couldn't get my head around the fact that after five years apart, the two of us were back in one another's lives again. Every detail of life with her felt brand new. My time of longing for her had been so much a part of me that now I wanted to slow down, savor the moments one at a time, let her presence fill that void. I knew my life was no longer simply my own as I discovered what Chesterton was describing when he wrote, "[T]here are no words to express the abyss between isolation and having one ally. It may be conceded to the mathematicians that four is twice two. But two is not twice one; two is two thousand times one."[1]

1. Chesterton, *The Man Who Was Thursday*, 65.

55

Erika and I liked to talk about the intricate details of our story—being teenagers and falling in love so easily and deeply, our years of separation, the long line of what had felt like random, unimportant decisions and events that had eventually led to our reunion and marriage—and the more we talked, the more like a fairy tale it all seemed. We talked about our rings as symbols of our vows, but our love seemed more like a fine watch: intricate, precious, and fragile. How it worked was mostly unseen except by the two of us—we knew what had gone into making it. In a watch, even a tiny filament of dust or a microscopic grain of sand interferes with the movements of the springs and gears, making it lose time; likewise, we knew that in our love, even small, unresolved arguments and misunderstandings could eventually seize our marriage and bring it to a standstill. We tried to keep our love clean, to sort out small differences and minor hurts. When we argued, we always did our best to keep our emotions in check and chose our words carefully, unable to imagine ongoing fights or the residue of lasting hurt or division between us. Blissful newlyweds, we told each other all of our old secrets, and swore we wouldn't let anything get in the way of our passionate love.

After three months of setting up house Erika got a job as a nurse at a hospital while I kept working at a daycare. We paid our bills and kept a bit of money for luxuries like going out for a meal now and then and watching movies. But after that, everything we earned and everything we had saved went towards paying off our student loans as quickly as we could. Like most newlyweds we didn't need much to live on, but we felt rich.

After our first anniversary, I wanted to buy Erika a watch. I knew we couldn't afford it, so on the weekends that she worked, I walked around our neighborhood, knocking on people's doors and offering to rake and bag the leaves in their yards with a borrowed rake from our building manager and a box of big orange garbage bags. When I picked up Erika after her evening shifts, I told her I had spent the day working on her gift, trying to give ambiguous hints, giddy that I was secretly earning a gift for her with my own hands, knocking on strangers' doors, raking clumps of wet leaves, fighting off fall's chill with hard work that gave me blisters and made my clothes and boots smell like a rotting garden. It felt like the best job I'd ever had. After about a month the snow came to stay and my secret job came to an end, but by then I had a jar full of bills and coins, hidden away in my desk drawer. Like a little boy with his piggy bank, I counted it all up, recounted it, and counted it again, and one day while she was at work, I went to a jewelry store and bought her a beautiful Swiss watch.

We celebrated Christmas, with just two gifts under our little tree, the evening before going to spend time with her family. When she opened the watch, she looked shocked and said, "We can't afford this." When I told her the story about how I had been working to earn the money for it, that it was all "bonus" money that wouldn't affect anything else we had to pay for, she cried, and I felt like a prince.

The following summer we moved to Vancouver so I could go back to school full-time. Erika found another nursing job and she also took a secret part-time job, cleaning house for a woman once a week, and when she had saved up enough money, she bought me a beautiful Swiss Army watch. I still wear it every day, a reminder and symbol of our love.

But eventually, the sweet, intoxicating "in-loveness" we had felt for one another as newlyweds, the passion that had seemed like it would never end, started to fade. As the differences between us grew, we realized how different from one another we had been all along. We got comfortable and careless, often unkind, and started taking one another for granted. We fought about petty differences and picked at each other over trivial things, sometimes fighting for what seemed like no reason at all.

It scared the hell out of me. We had such a beautiful love story and we had done all we could to keep our love running smoothly— keeping short records with one another, talking through our differences, sorting out our conflicts quickly—but we were running into problems that neither of us could solve. It felt like we were falling apart, turning out to be just like every disheartening, discouraging stereotype of a married couple: distant, chilly, quarrelsome, barely tolerant of one another. I thought that our conflicts were a sign of some deeper failure, a relational malfunction that needed to be fixed. I wanted to get inside the mechanics of our marriage and find the problem, make the necessary repairs and adjustments, then set our love back into motion again.

Now it is possible that my desire to "fix" the problems in our marriage was, in part, a reflection of a stereotypically male bias: the gadget-loving, wannabe handyman who thinks nearly every problem can be fixed with a pair of visegrips, a table saw, and some duct tape. But I think my sense of a "mechanical failure" was a symptom of a broader misconception, namely that we humans have come to see ourselves as nothing more than complex machines, like fleshy computers. "There is a reduction," writes Wendell Berry, "that seems endemic to modern science, and from science it has spread everywhere. I mean the definition or identification of the world and all its creatures as 'machines.'"[2] The metaphor, according to his argument, has evolved into an ideology, and increasingly we are encouraged to think of our human problems as "mechanical failures" and assume that these can be "fixed" by trained specialists and experts.

Unwanted fat can be removed by a machine, hair loss restored by laser beams, and a sagging erection fixed with a little blue pill. More and more we think of ourselves as "specimens" says Berry, subject to the towering powers of science. "The specialist to whom you have been 'referred' may never have seen you before, may know nothing about you, and may never see you again, and yet he or she presumes to know exactly what is wrong with you."[3] They are total strangers whom we nonetheless trust to make our bodies function as they ought to.

If there are specialists to fix our physical bodies—technicians to fix the hardware—there are also specialists trained to fix our minds and spirits—technicians to fix the software. Whatever emotional or relational problems we might have, they are technical concerns, glitches in the programming, coding errors in the operating system, and once the source of the trouble has been located and fixed, our internal machines should run smoothly. Marriage counselors help husbands and wives "interface" and overcome communication errors, like fleshy networking. They might tell the couple that their various parts are incompatible, and that they should both look for someone who operates on the same platform.

I trust that some of these specialists have their place, and I am certainly grateful for the health experts who know about infections and surgeries and the products and procedures that are available to help treat me when I am truly sick. But I resist the ideology of abstraction and specialization that tells us that we are machines and that our

2. Berry, *Life Is a Miracle*, 46.

3. Ibid., 40.

lack of expertise leaves us unqualified to treat ourselves. The problem with the need to fix is that you cannot possibly *fix* a living thing—and a relationship is as much a living thing as the individuals who are a part of it. There is no operator's manual for a marriage, no scientifically proven technique that can tell you all you need to know about the particulars of your life, your spouse, or your relationship. The authors and professionals who presume to promise us ease because they know how to make love safe and relationships more predictable, those who treat marriage as a sort of simple equation, are hawkers of expensive and dangerously misleading nonsense.

Love is fundamentally grounded in mystery. Erika and I live and act in ignorance, smack-dab in the middle of mystery, never knowing precisely what we are doing, but committing together to love one another as best we can. Even though we still don't know how our relationship really "works," we are learning how to cultivate and nurture love so that our marriage can survive and hopefully thrive.

Last summer, Erika and I grew our first real garden. We both come from rural families, but neither of us had ever grown a garden before. We discovered that our ignorance didn't disqualify us from trying. We turned the soil, planted some seeds and seedlings, pulled weeds, watched, and waited. I planted the potatoes with the sense that I had certainly done it wrong but they all grew, every one of them. We picked off the potato bugs when they arrived, then picked them again and again. Eventually we dug up our first potato plant and feasted on steamed potatoes with butter. When summer came we watched the plants blossom and the fruit begin to grow. As things began to ripen, we picked bags and bags of green beans and cucumbers, and we waited for the tomatoes to turn red. In September we dug up hundreds of pounds of potatoes and carrots and onions, picked fat ears of corn and bags of peas, and when the tomatoes finally got ripe, we stayed up late every night for a week blanching them and canning them for the winter. Our harvest felt like a true miracle.

Likewise, our love—tended and cared for as best but imperfectly as we can—grows by mystery, watched over by God, more miracle than machine. I'm learning to trust the poets before the scientists because poets spend their lives making room for miracles. A tomato is a miracle; love, too. Only love—up-close, personal, committed, engaged, involved—will do, for both the means and the end is love. When our

love bears fruit, we wait for it to ripen, watching with anticipation, doing our best to look after it, and when we taste the fruit, we are amazed
to discover that it is more delicious and abundant than we ever could
have imagined.

Why Love

Will Always Be

a Poor Investment

We cannot be too careful about the words we use; we start out using them and then they end up using us. 'Consumer' is the catch-all term for the way we are viewed. For those of us who are reared in North American culture, it is inevitable that we should unconsciously acquire this way of looking at everyone we meet.

—Eugene Peterson,
Christ Plays in Ten Thousand Places

Contemporary western culture is so thoroughly saturated with the values and assumptions of the corporate world that it comes as no surprise that we now construct even our understanding of romantic relationships in economic terms:

1. Where once a person had a boyfriend or girlfriend, husband or wife, we now refer to one's significant other as a "partner." As with the corporation partner in the business world, the partner in a relationship is presumably always on the lookout for the best deal, the partnership that will maximize his or her interests.

61

2. Time spent with a partner is considered investing in the relationship. Investment has replaced out-of-date notions like loyalty, commitment or responsibility, and an individual's primary responsibility is to protect his or her interests.

3. Like any good financial investment, a relational investment ought to provide the investor with calculable and escalating returns.

4. In our progressive, open-market partnerships, we pride ourselves for having moved beyond encumbering, old-fashioned marriage; therefore, any partnership can be abandoned if the current one is too demanding, if the returns are too low, or if a better option happens to present itself.

5. Anyone who notices a trend of diminishing returns on their investment in their partnership should choose what's best for them, which may mean opting out of the agreement.

6. In order to guard against the vulnerabilities of a relationship, partners are well advised to sign a pre-nuptial agreement before they get married. The pre-nup contract carefully delineates the divvying up of the material possessions and guardianship of children should the partnership ever be dissolved.

7. Ideally, these contracts mean that the termination of a partnership should be tidy, logical, and efficient. Partners can avoid the stereotypical "messy" divorce by following the step-by-step details of the mutually agreed upon terms of the binding contract.

Now, there have never been any "good old days" of marriage. Some of today's most vocal proponents of traditional marriage speak as though it was during the days of their courtship that the standard for proper and holy marriage was set. According to them, it seems that God finally ironed out the wrinkles and perfected the ideal marriage somewhere in America, sometime during the 1950s. "In those days," men worked hard at their jobs and in church and prayed with, impregnated, and protected their pious wives who stayed home to tend to the domestic duties that the pursuit of happiness entailed. And God had never been more pleased with all those perfect marriages!

I stand *with* those who stand *against* the narrow, dehumanizing roles that this sort of traditional marriage often created for women and for men. Appealing to the values of utopian "good old days" often means returning to an era riddled with institutionally sanctioned injustice. Many of the things that happened behind the closed doors of these good Christian homes were anything but Christian, and the stamp of supposedly divine approval does not make oppression and patriarchy any less oppressive or patriarchal.

But it seems to me that the relationship-as-commodity mentality, rather than the fear of the abuses of traditional marriage, has done much more to foster today's general mood of suspicion towards lifelong commitment. Though the backlash against the abuses of the traditional family has caused many of my generation to write off life-long marriage as unrealistic, out-of-date, or oppressive, most of us still marry, yet it is less and less likely that we will stay in the relationship for life. "Love, honor, and cherish, 'till death do us part" is an archaism, like manual typewriters and 78 RPM records: some people still seem to enjoy those sorts of things, but probably only if they subscribe to some resurgent vein of Luddite thinking.

Now that we can choose from among the dozens of different kinds of toothpaste or hundreds of television channels, free to pick and choose what kind of designer coffee to drink and which partner— or exotic sexual encounter—suits our tastes or interests or desires, we are told we are free. But things have not turned out as we might have hoped. I have yet to hear anyone argue convincingly that our culture is more characterized by genuine love than it was fifty years ago. The presumed right to be free to sleep with a different person every night of the week might very well be mistaken for genuine freedom, but it will never be mistaken for genuine love.

Love defies measurement, technique, and all guarantees of ease and comfort. Love is fundamentally anti-program, non-rational, and impractical. Love is an untamable impediment to the march of progress; it defies the promises of professionally developed technique, creates inefficiency, and does not guarantee "escalating returns" on "investments." What it does guarantee is challenge, struggle, sorrow,

fame

and loss. Love is what human beings live for, and like Aslan the Lion, it is not safe, but it is good.

Take, for example, Kevin and Laura, a couple who gave me one of the purest examples of how love is eminently good but not safe. After meeting in graduate school, they started dating, fell in love, and got engaged in the span of four months, only to discover that Laura was suffering from Stage 4 bone and lymph node cancer. The doctors laid out a spectrum of treatment options, ranging from intensive chemotherapy and radiation to "maintenance" by natural medicine, all with the understanding that none of these would cure her, only prolong her life with varying degrees of bodily damage. The prognosis was that she would likely not live more than two or three more years.

Now. Any reasonable, investment-minded couple would have carefully considered their options, weighed the costs and benefits of proceeding as planned, and called the wedding off. But Kevin and Laura chose instead to plunge themselves deeper into the insecurity and guaranteed suffering of genuine love: knowing that time was short, they bumped up the wedding date and got married two months earlier than they had originally planned. They never got far beyond newlyweds: in the end, they had less than three years together before Laura died.

The example these two have set shows precisely how the commitment to one person "till death do us part" in the vow of marriage is truly a poor investment. Whether you end up like Kevin and Laura with only a few years together, or manage to sashay through to your sixty-fifth anniversary, barring some accident that takes you both at once, one of you is going to outlive the other. And the longer the two of you stay together and pour love into one another's lives, the greater the sorrow will be when one of you dies. What then? What reasonable, economic explanation is there for a grieving lover? What words of calculable comfort can one offer the widow or widower? What consolation is there for this sort of return on their investment?

In a culture where everything is supposedly for sale, the implicit understanding of love-as-commodity is that love is scarce and that you need gather up as much of it as you can. But the kind of love that Kevin and Laura lived by is freely offered to another rather than greedily hoarded for oneself. The underlying message of covenantal love is: I commit myself to sharing my life with you in a way that furthers *your* well-being. Love in marriage is mutual self-giving, the back-and-forth sharing of a gift which cannot be measured. Covenantal love always trusts and hopes, and it always perseveres.

When I pledged my vows to Erika ten years ago, I promised to love her "until death separates us." I offered my life for the sake of hers, and she pledged the same to me; now my well-being is her well-being is my well-being. By saying this one "yes" to marriage, I also said "no" to a long line of other options. I gave up the freedom to "consume," because I chose to love this one person, not simply until the returns began to diminish, but to the very end.

Like every doe-eyed newlywed, it didn't take long for the two of us to discover that love in the day-to-day isn't all bliss. More than the petty arguments about which way to hang the toilet paper roll or whose turn it is to do the dishes, what was as painful as it was beautiful was simply being known. Erika is like an honest mirror that reveals to me who I really am. She encourages me to foster my strengths, but she also helps me to see my weaknesses. She sees me very clearly, and like every normal human being, I have plenty that I would prefer to keep all to myself. But ignoring my fundamentally unhealthy ways of living is no more helpful than ignoring a tumour: it doesn't go away, and it doesn't get any better. Love brings to light my diseased ways of living and says: "Look, some of these things are really quite bad, but all is not lost; we still have hope for you. The thing is we will need to do some major surgery, and it's going to hurt. But there is really no other way that you're going to get well."

Each time that this sort of diagnosis occurs I have, as far as I can see, three options: the first is divorce, which would supposedly be a quick and permanent solution. But if I cut and run, I still haven't dealt with the illness. I'm still sick. Besides, Erika and I made a commitment to a lifelong relationship. We're stuck; there is no getting out. This brings me to the second option, which is to do nothing at all, to ignore every challenge and simply let the marriage take whatever course it chooses, which will inevitably lead to a miserable relationship. I have known too many couples who refused to take the steps that love asked them to, who lived with their personal and relational diseases because it was easier than making a painful change. There is a cold comfort in a familiar malady, even when you know it's killing you. This leaves me, then, with a third option—the riskiest of them all, which is why plenty of people opt for either of the first two—to plunge into absurd love, into the uncertainty of the changes that love asks me to make.

The commitment to lifelong love provides a crucible that burns off the dross and refines the gold of the human soul. There are no shortcuts, and the only guarantee is that it will hurt. The longer that two people work on their absurd love, the more they will one day hurt.

Sometimes at night, just before Erika and I fall asleep, we talk about this sort of thing (when we should probably be praying), confessing to one another that we don't know if we have what it would take to survive without the other. It's sobering and it seems morbid, but it's realistic. Death will come, someday. And now that we have two young kids in the mix, the thought of losing each other is even more painful and the risks of continuing to love are even greater. What should we do? Cut our losses and get out before it hurts even more? Start making ourselves safer and less vulnerable? Or continue doing all we can to deepen what we have, and continue to love each other in a way that ensures that we *will* suffer?

My maternal grandmother died when I was only nine. Her husband, my grandfather, outlived her by thirteen years, but he never got over her. I used to imagine that it must somehow hurt less to lose a long-married spouse late in life. But now I believe that love makes holes in peoples hearts, and the longer you love, the deeper the holes. And when the husband or wife dies, all those holes that love made fill up with the lover's absence. The heart fills with pools of grief. To love is to grieve. But I have no interest in trying to make it through life without scars, and I'm not going to run. I will stay. If there is no way to escape the risk of love, there is nothing else I would rather risk everything for. Even if love one day fills my heart full of grief, it is still the only thing worth living for.

I am married. For good.

In Cupped Hands

To me, news of a divorce is almost as hard-hitting as news of a death. So when my father told me that old friends of our family were filing for divorce after nearly thirty years of marriage, I was shocked because they hadn't seemed like a couple heading for failure. Even though their relationship never struck me as extraordinary, I had assumed that their marriage was much like everyone's, held together by an endless number of bonds formed in the small details of everyday life together—moments in the kitchen and backyard and bedroom, in all the arguments and reconciliation, conflicts and forgiveness—all the things that only the two of them would ever know about. These unspectacular everyday moments are the things that bind Erika and me to each other, like threads in the weave of a cloth. Marriage certainly has intense moments, for better and for worse, but for the most part married living isn't anything extraordinary; it's everyday.

So with the news of any divorce, as I fret about what happened, I wonder: how are we going to make it? The looming enemies of love—resentment, grudges, deceit, divisiveness, unforgiveness, selfishness, unfaithfulness—are the same enemies that all lovers face and that every lasting couple has to fight against. But I know that I am susceptible to the same marriage-breaking temptations that have seduced husbands who have seemed stronger than I am. I am not immune to the diseases that kill love, so how will I be able to follow through on my vow, my promise to love Erika until death separates us? How will our marriage survive what is ahead? What must we do to be saved?

And at the same time, what must we *not* do? Sometimes Erika and I fight dirty. Sometimes it seems like we are held together more by a desire to win an argument than by the love we promised one another. We fight without offering forgiveness, create boundaries like border lines, defend as simply hers or mine what we vowed we would share as ours. And sometimes, too, we're madly in love, passionate for each other, as blissful as when we first started dating. Maybe these are just the sorts of rhythms and changes that every relationship goes through. In one of his poems, Wendell Berry describes his enjoyment of the "immemorial" cycles of life:

> hunger, thirst,
> their satisfaction; work-weariness,
> earned rest; the falling again
> from loneliness to love[1]

It's possible that our fights are normal, and there is really no need to worry because we're doing fine, and we, too, will fall again "from loneliness to love." The heavy seasons of even our worst arguments have always passed, at least so far. But what if we run into a bitter season that stretches on without passing? What if we fall into loneliness and stay there?

In the small, rural community where I grew up, one of my good friends, who was a few years older than me, was as much a farmer as any of his peers, but he was also interested in painting, playing guitar, writing songs and poetry and reading. When I was an awkward teenager he encouraged me to cultivate a healthy restlessness, a hunger to know about the world beyond what we could see right around us. When he got married, I was in grade twelve, and he asked me to be a groomsman.

1. Berry, "Goods," 200.

But four years later, he called me up from halfway across the country and wept as he told me that he and his wife were separated and filing for a divorce. "I made a mistake. I married the wrong woman," he told me, and went on to explain that he had pushed aside the gifts God had given him to get married. Now, rather than settle for the dissatisfaction of a lifelong, miserable relationship, they were going their separate ways.

A year later, after a judge put the official stamp of approval on their divorce, a group of us gathered around a campfire one night, and I asked him if the divorce had threatened his faith, wondering if he felt like God had let him down. But he took it as an attack and said that I was just like everyone else who had assumed that if he got a divorce he must have also turned his back on God. He had heard that a lot already. Even though I felt misunderstood, I didn't try to straighten it out with him because I could see that his wounds were still raw.

Yet every time I hear that another marriage has ended in divorce, it feels like a betrayal, a break in faith. Five, ten, twenty, thirty years farther down the same journey that Erika and I are on, these husbands and wives are sending back this report: *We couldn't do it; marriage didn't work for us. Best of luck. You're going to need it.*

It seems to me that divorce is more than just two people turning their backs on one another; they are turning their backs on marriage itself. It makes me want to fight back and say, *How dare you walk away from this thing that is still so dear to me.* I am still staking everything on love, on my vow to love and honor and respect Erika, with death as the only final fulfillment. In the play, *A Man for All Seasons,* Thomas More says that whatever vows we take are spoken to God. Arguing with his family, who is trying to convince him to take back a vow in order to save his life, he says, "When a man takes an oath . . . he's holding his own self in his own hands. Like water . . . and if he opens his fingers *then*—he needn't hope to find himself again."[2]

Like the soon-to-be martyred priest in the play, all of history's husbands and wives hold ourselves in cupped hands. In marriage, we all take the same vow, all participate in the same love, all bind ourselves in faith to a good that is greater and more mysterious than any of us could ever comprehend. "By staying," says Wendell Berry, "and only by staying, we will learn something of the truth, that the truth is

2. Bolt, *A Man For All Seasons,* 83.

good to know, and that it is always both different and larger than we thought."[3] Marriage will always be stronger, deeper, more surprising, renewing and mysterious than any of us who enter into it; it is, after all, God's idea. It holds no less strength for a husband and wife today than it did for the first husband and wife in Eden. We are not the makers of marriage; we are participants in it. Every time someone walks away from that, the problem is not that love was not big enough, but that someone has willfully chosen to shut the doors to love.

Returning to the old friends of our family getting divorced after thirty years of marriage: what discord were they tending instead of seeds of love, that they would harvest such bitter, withered fruit? How did they take three decades of conversations, arguments, sex, work, kids, homes, afternoon naps, forgiveness, taxes, breakfasts, lunches, dinners, neighbors, laundry, vacations, and reduce it to "There's nothing there, we have nothing in common"?

Falling out of love is inevitable, even for the so-called "perfect couples," but you fall back into love again, by a good deal of hard work, of course, and through those gracious gifts which are among God's greatest treasures: humility, forgiveness, and grace. But you will not fall back into love if you do not stay.

When my dad talked with his friend, the husband told him, "If we met each other now, we would never get married." And I want to tell this man what a frivolous, imaginary game he is playing because he is who he is precisely because he has spent the last thirty years being married to his wife. The self he has is the self he has been given over the last three decades. "Marriage has not failed you," I want to tell him. "You have failed marriage."

I know I'm being defensive. I need to defend marriage because I need to defend *my* marriage. Like all things guarded and protected by love, my marriage is strong, but it is still vulnerable—even a hundred-year-old oak tree can be poisoned. I feel threatened when others whom I admire don't make it. But I'm strengthened and encouraged by those who hang on like endangered species. As one professor said the week before celebrating his fortieth anniversary, "There have definitely been times when it would have been much *easier* for the two of us to go our own ways and simply call it quits." He paused. "But staying together has meant that life is so much *richer*."

3. Berry, "Poetry and Marriage," 98.

Despite my uncertainty about how my marriage will survive, I will not live under the burden of the fear that Erika and I might not have what it takes to make it. I won't live as if love is ultimately meaningless, no more than a mechanism of biological necessity, or an illusion. In our ten years of marriage, though we have had times when it would have been easier to give up, we also have learned the richness of staying. So this is it: I'm staying, and so is she.

And, yet, with all the tenacity and resolve we can muster, we still tremble as we pray: "Heaven, help us."

'A Heart I Love'

On his 1975 album *Nighthawks at the Diner*, Tom Waits sings like he's got the world by the tail. Only four years into his recording career, Waits was already a highly esteemed songwriter whose carefully honed persona—a cross between bohemian beatnik and drunken hobo, simultaneously celebrating the excesses and indulgences of the unfettered artist who says "yes" to nearly every opportunity to broaden his experience, while vividly portraying the lonely, sorrowful underbelly that was its flipside—was equal parts fact and fiction. In "Better Off Without a Wife" Waits celebrates going out whenever he wants and sleeping "'till the crack of noon," but the last verse reveals the lonely part of the story: "Selfish about my privacy/as long as I can be with me/we get along so well I can't believe."[1] Waits' lifestyle—an emulation of a version of freedom espoused by the likes of Bukowski, Kerouac, and Ginsberg, and the crowd that followed them—fed his creative side. A year after *Nighthawks*, he took a room at the Tropicana motel and ended up staying for nearly three years. He loved the nightlife. He loved to

---

1. Waits, "Better Off Without A Wife."

drink, had a long string of lovers and girlfriends who fell for his persona as much as for him, and he loved to follow whatever experience might come his way, no matter where it took him. But even on that same record he strips the sentimental veneer off the lifestyle; the "high tonight" was inevitably followed by the lonely and "low tomorrow, with precipitation expected."[2]

But in 1981, a bright young Catholic woman named Kathleen Brennan followed a hint from a friend and knocked on the door of the studio where Waits was frantically trying to write songs for a Francis Ford Coppola film. When Waits answered the door, Brennan asked, "What are you doing?" "I'm writing songs," he said. "Who are *you*?" It was love at first sight, he said later. "I opened the door and there she was and that was it."[3] Waits was smitten by Kathleen's poise and striking beauty, and within a week they were engaged. In 1983 Waits released *Swordfishtrombones,* a mixed up musical ride that sounds like circus music, campfire storytelling, 20's jazz, and weird dreams. Unlike anything Waits had done before, its musical strangeness signified a new beginning and from then on, Waits started splitting songwriting credits with Kathleen, his wife.

Waits refutes the pervasive and bleak sentimental stereotype that creativity can only thrive in personal chaos or self-destructiveness or that lifelong love is anathema to the creative process. According to Waits' biographer Barney Hoskyns, it was Kathleen who inspired Waits to try new musical ideas, developed his songwriting, and encouraged him to write music for theatre.[4] His old musical colleagues and drinking companions seemed to resent Kathleen, blaming her for the fact that the old Tom they used to get stupid-drunk with wasn't around anymore. Waits, who was already fairly private about his personal life, became like a protective grizzly bear: those rare moments when you actually saw him, unless you knew him really well, you didn't want to get too close.

Anyone who's been married for very long knows that it takes an awful lot of time and effort to keep a marriage functioning, let alone healthy, and if you listen to much of the music they make together, it's clear that Tom is still in love with Kathleen. Unlike the best kinds of

2. Tom Waits, "Emotional Weather Report."

3. Hoskyns, *Lowside of the Road,* 245.

4. Ibid., 272, 327.

houseplants—or my in-laws' car—marriages don't thrive on neglect. Throw kids into the mix, and the required commitments of time and effort increase exponentially. When Waits and Brennan had their third child, Waits took three full years off from touring and recording to stay home and change diapers and drive the older kids to school in the Chevy Suburban, not the sort of thing one would expect from an artist. "I adore my wife and kids," he says. Waits' sons, Casey and Sullivan, record and tour with him now, and Kathleen still co-writes the majority of songs he records. His old friends may still lament the long-lost Tom; as a husband and a father of two young kids, I cheer for the guy. He grew up. He left behind his boozing and swinging, and he learned to cleave to his wife. "There's a notion that artists are kind of impetuous and eccentric and irresponsible and unreliable," says Waits. "But I don't think you have to be."[5]

Despite his secrecy about his personal life, Waits described the song, "Take It With Me," as very vulnerable. "We wrote that one together, Kathleen and I, and it felt good. Two people who are in love writing a song about being in love."[6] Waits, who, on some songs, barks and howls like a lunatic in a bad dream, barely breathes out the lines in this one, like an old man who's given up on his youthful folly and resigned himself to let love take him on a journey all its own. In the last verse of the song, Waits' poetic camera zooms in on more and more concrete details, narrowing his focus until we get to the beating heart of his song, the center of his work and life:

> In a land there's a town
> And in that town there's a house
> And in that house there's a woman
> And in that woman there's a heart I love
> I'm gonna take it with me when I go.[7]

It is almost unheard of for a famous musician to sing a love song for the same woman he fell in love with nearly thirty years ago, but it's Waits' roles as husband and family man as much as his music that make me admire him.

5. Ibid., 411.
6. Schoemer, "More Dylan than Dylan."
7. Waits, "Take It With Me."

PART
THREE

Grace

Bring Your Toothbrush to the Avalanche

CHAPTER 12

I'm lying in bed, fuming.

Sometimes it seems like Erika and I are so entirely incompatible, so perfectly mismatched that we might have been better off not getting married at all. Sometimes it seems like the days we try to spend together as a family are the hardest, and maybe it's easier and better if I spend most of the day at work and out of the house. I want to be rational, but right now, in the thick of it, I am far too angry.

Today started to go badly over small things, minor disappointments about unspoken and unmet expectations for what our day would be like. My early hours of reading were interrupted when the kids woke up way too early and wouldn't go back to sleep, and because I'm such a generous husband and magnanimous father, I tried to keep the kids quiet and fed so Erika could sleep in, so I made pancakes and read library books and got the two of them dressed for the day and was feeling generous and magnanimous, but by the time she woke up the pancakes were cold and soggy and I was pretending I wasn't hurt and angry. The kids fought in the living room every time I went to the kitchen to try to clean up, and I threatened to send them to their rooms, which seemed to help them get along better, but made me tense. Then the two of them put up such a stink when we tried to get them dressed to go outside to play in the snow that I once again threatened to send them to their rooms, which, of course, completely backfired because that sounded just fine to them since neither of them wanted to go outside in the first place. I'm certain they would behave better if I was the one staying home with them. So we were only outside for about five minutes when Molly said, "I have to pee," and I went back inside with her and helped her take off her mitts, scarf, boots, and snowsuit, helped her in the bathroom, helped her get dressed again, meanwhile Jack's outside wrestling with the neighbor boys and Erika is clearly having a relaxing morning, which makes me even more upset because so far my morning sucks. When we get back outside I asked her if she was still planning to run errands in the afternoon and she said yes and I got grumpy and quiet because I want to go out and do my errands, too, and when she asked me, "What's wrong?" I lied and said, "Nothing," and kept being quiet and grumpy until it was obvious to everyone, including our kids and the neighbors and their kids and probably even Molly's pet fish upstairs, that something was clearly wrong, but if she couldn't just figure out for herself what the real problem was, I wasn't about to tell her.

And when we all came inside the kids put up a stink again and whined about having to put their winter things away so I sent them to their rooms, which freed up Erika and I to argue about what to make for lunch, and that stupid little fight finally somehow pushed both of us too far, and we spent the rest of the day in a very prolonged argument, where every word, every phrase, every look, every calculated moment of silence, even the pace and thump of our footsteps, carried a very deliberate barb. I fought with her in my imagination even when we weren't saying anything, and she gave me the "I'm-fighting-with-you-in-my-head" look at least a dozen times. I made a lame attempt to reconcile ("Look, Erika, I'm really not trying to be difficult"), but it only made things worse ("I'm not saying you're trying, but it's still turning out that way").

By mid-afternoon we were dredging up old hurts and fears, caught up in the Big Endless Fight we've been having for years: we are, in countless ways, impossibly different from one another. And now it's like today's arguments have triggered an avalanche of snow, and we're both fighting to stay ahead of the other. It's a race to the bottom.

And so I'm lying here in bed, grumpy, replaying anger like a scratched CD that's been skipping for hours, and she has just walked away from my brooding silence to brush her teeth, of all things. What does she think she's doing, walking away like that, starting an avalanche and then abandoning me in the middle of it as though nothing's wrong. It's our problem, not just mine. We've got to deal with this roaring wall of snow and ice blasting towards us at a hundred miles an hour.

I really want to just ignore this and wait for it to pass. Other couples do this sort of thing all the time, go to bed in the middle of a fight, argue until they're too tired to stay awake, then roll over, turn off the light, and sleep it off. I'm sure things are lighter come morning. Maybe we could just ignore each other until we get to sleep. But I know I could never fall asleep when I'm this anxious.

I'm trying to work out my side of the argument and I'm starting to realize I'm being foolish, but right now nothing about this feels foolish. Petty frustrations have turned to deep anger, and we've found ourselves in the middle of an unfinished battle. As is often the case, we've moved from the trivial to the apocalyptic.

I can picture exactly what she's doing in the bathroom: the click of her toothbrush in the cup, the creak of the medicine cabinet door for the dental floss, the different tones of the singing hot water pipes as she finds just the right temperature. I know all the sounds of her nighttime routines. And while she is getting ready for bed, I'm here engaged in the argument in my head, scripting perfect arguments for why I'm justified for being angry, and how everything would be fine if she would just acknowledge that. My lines are fantastic. I craft pointed, clever one-liners—"You act as though clean teeth are more important than a clean marriage"—brilliant and effective, because as the imaginary argument continues, Erika understands just how right I am. I have just the right response for everything she says, and I express myself clearly and with just the right amount of righteous anger. Gradually, she comes to see things from my point of view. Really, she ought to be grateful to be married to a guy like me, so kind and generous, moral, rational, right more often than not. I think I'll remind her of that: just think of what it would be like if you'd married so-and-so.

I'll walk her through the day, step by step, and we'll sort the whole thing out smoothly. She'll appreciate how rational and coherent I am and will come to understand me perfectly.

I hear her open the bathroom door, and walk back towards our room.

In an instant my confidence disappears. She opens the bedroom door, turns out the light, and crawls into bed, but keeps her distance.

Most of what I know about how to sort out conflict I learned from people on television—characters like Fred and Wilma Flintstone, Cliff and Claire Huxtable and all the good looking kids on Beverly Hills 90210. My lessons from the television couples made it seem like fighting should be fairly straightforward:

- Right off the start, it should be obvious who is right and who is wrong.

- Anyone who fights for good and noble reasons—integrity, freedom, tolerance, or being true to their self—is always right.

- Arguments should proceed smoothly, but with plenty of drama.

- Both sides should argue eloquently, each one's rationality undisturbed by passionate feelings, even in the most heated conflict.

- Fighting should involve perfect self-expression, two exemplary individuals arguing and fighting while their independence and individuality remain intact.

- Even if the right side doesn't win, we should know without any real doubt who's right and who's wrong.

- Every argument should have a clear resolution.

Of course, TV actors recite lines from a carefully edited and rehearsed script, the key moments constructed with just the right music and lighting, which is why television arguments always leave me in a more pleasant mood than my own arguments do.

My parents only sorted out minor disagreements in front of us kids, so for most of my years at home, it seemed like their relationship was nearly perfect. From what I could see, they never had any serious conflict or difficulties. I know better now, because conflict is inevitable in any close relationship. I know that they must have had plenty of arguments, just not in front of us. Recently I asked my mom why they kept their conflict so private, and she said that the two of them argued mostly about sex and how to raise us kids. They didn't think those arguments were appropriate for us to hear.

Erika and I take pride in the fact that we get along well—much better than some couples we know—but we still argue a lot. We can fight about the right way to chop an onion, or whose turn it is to get up with the kids in the middle of the night, and we've had some remarkably heated arguments about which movie to rent or whether or not our kids need to wear scarves to go outside. We bicker over details, the small, everyday things, which is frustrating because our lives are made up mostly of small, everyday things. At the café where I used to work, one of my favorite regulars was ordering his usual cup of coffee, and I overheard him telling stories from his years in the Air Force during World War I. "Being up in the plane," he said, "well, mostly it's very, very boring, just very routine. Nothing happens. Nothing at all. But every now and then there are a handful of moments of absolute terror." Sounds familiar.

When Erika fights, she has no trouble coming up with something to say. She fights hot, like a pile of small sticks on fire, and she argues like she's driving a bulldozer, trying to finish up a demolition job as the machine is about to run out of fuel. I can never guess what she's going to say. Her words are fast, unscripted, and uncensored, jumping back and forth between defense and offense. She says whatever she needs to until she feels better, and once she has everything off her chest, she feels fine again.

I get lost in complicated, conflicted emotions that are usually too muddled to articulate. I can't think in the middle of conflict. My feelings are so heavy, so intense, it feels like there's something physically pressing on my chest. It's too much to put into words, so I silently brood, sometimes for hours, sometimes for days, and I start making lists of grievances and hurts that have been going unnoticed but now suddenly seem like terrible injustices. All those little things—it's not my turn to clean the bathroom, and what did you do with that stack of books I was working on, and aw, come on, did you really snack on that dish of leftovers that I set aside for tomorrow's lunch?—become major offences, like she's doing everything she can to bug me.

There is no clear resolution, no right and wrong, no end-credits to wait for. We are simply at odds, holding onto resentments, waiting for a chance to throw in an uncaring, sarcastic jab or cruel criticism. We know one another's weaknesses better than anyone else does, and when we fight, those are the first places we aim for. Our fights over the small things pull us into the greater challenges posed by our serious differences—unresolved hurt feelings and old insecurities, stress about our roles as parents, worries about money, fears that, despite our best hopes, we do not know what it means to live well—all of which we are most poignantly aware of when we're at odds with one another. It's a dirty game, and it hurts. I never know how we're going to make our way out of it.

Over the years, we've learned that, for the endless number of things we argue over, there seems to be one basic issue at the core of nearly all of our conflict, from the petty arguments to the full-scale battles: we're afraid of not getting what we think we really need. Both of us are afraid of losing, of sacrificing what is vital to ourselves and not getting what we need in return. For all that Erika and I have in common, for all the love we give to one another, the shared history we have, the common story the two of us are learning to work on together, we are still two different people. Marriage may be a holy union, a mysterious "one," but there's no escaping that there are still two of us, she and I. Both of us still like having things our own way.

I have seen other marriages scarred by conflict, wrecked by the deep-rooted bitterness of decades-old conflicts left unresolved and unhealed, the kind of discord that sets husband and wife continuously against one another. Their differences become a wall of bitterness that destroys the love that brought them together in the first place. I know I have the potential for the same sort of resentment that turns passionate lovers into vicious enemies.

But the goal in marriage is not victory, but love, and the only way to get there is through love. Love doesn't leave room for trying to come out on top or for holding onto resentment or selfish grudges. Love doesn't tolerate the arbitrary divisions that we sometimes try to maintain. Every hurt is an opportunity to draw a line, separating me from her, where one of us says, no longer will I cross over to you in openness. I now stand my ground, for the safety of my cherished individuality. Yet by my vow, I am called back to love, over and over again, to forgive as often as I am wronged, to learn to live with openness and vulnerability, to be wounded and offer forgiveness. "Love keeps no record of wrongs"—keeps no balance sheet, no long-standing list of grievances or debts. The invitation to forgive is endless because the hurts will never cease. We forgive, or our love will die.

It's cold in our room, late fall. Especially cold tonight, it seems.

We lie here, side by side, staring at the ceiling, and I whisper the only thing I can come up with: "You're not being fair." We used to make a habit of trying to hold hands when we were fighting, just so we would stay connected, close to each other, but it's become much harder to do that.

"Yeah, well, I'm hurt," she says.

Hang on, I'm the one who has been wronged here. I am supposed to say how I feel, and she's supposed to see how right I am, and then I'll be on to my quick victory. What's my line now?

"I hate fighting like this with you," I say. I feel like the character in Terry Taylor's song, who can never come up with something to say, especially when he needs to most. "But the answer I needed somehow wouldn't come/from the back of my mind to the tip of my tongue."[1]

She tells me her side of the story, why she is hurt, and my first reaction is to justify myself, plead innocence, because I'm not willing to give an inch, at least not yet. I'm hurt, too, and still angry. I want to hurt her back, make her admit that she was wrong. I start to ramble on, and it's not witty or brilliant, but messy and disjointed.

And then, somewhere in there, she lets down her guard. "I'm sorry," she says, turning her face towards me for the first time in hours.

Love hits me sideways. As we talk, I keep staring at the ceiling, and then she reaches out her hand to find mine. I turn to face her, and we inch closer. She slides her foot over and rests it on my leg. Her toes are cold. Reconciliation. Then forgiveness. "I love you, of course," she says. My tight-fisted grasp on my list of wrongs slips, and the pressure I felt on my chest lifts.

"I forgive you," I say, and as the wall between us crumbles, we find our way back to one another, back to love that is broad enough for the two of us and our trivial, terrifying, impossible differences.

1. Taylor, "What I Should Have Said."

Platitude, Cliché, Bla,

Incorruptible

Bla, Bla

CHAPTER 13

Why do we breathe and move and exist? Because of faith.
Without it, nothing at all would ever happen. Not even this
line I am writing now. This, for me, is absolutely true.

—David Adams Richards,
God Is

My hometown of Youngstown, Alberta
(pop. 300) had three places to get drunk on Saturday
night (including the seasonal bar in the community
curling rink) and three different churches to try to make
things right come Sunday morning. There was the tiny
Catholic church with chipped paint and grass that usually needed mowing and a bell tower whose bell I don't
remember hearing ring once, and there was the slightly
bigger United church, which had an Atco trailer pulled
up behind it to house the Sunday school classes. I had
friends from both the Catholic and United churches, but
judging by their stories about the drinking they did on
Saturday night, I never really believed that their churches
could be truly Christian. Any church that let people get
drunk couldn't be Christian. They were *religious* church-

es, and I didn't believe in religion. I believed in a personal *relationship* with Jesus. Religion was a hollow, empty ritual to try to please God; true Christian faith was about me and Jesus.

My family went to the Youngstown Gospel Chapel, which self-identified as "Evangelical" and "interdenominational," but which was strongly influenced by Plymouth Brethrens and deeply conservative in its theology and practice. As a little kid I learned that I was a sinner and that Jesus wanted my heart, and I gave mine to him when I was four, thus assuring myself that I would go to heaven when I died. The years of Sunday school and youth group taught me all I needed to know about how to be a good Christian: reading my bible and praying, going to youth group, being careful about what movies I watched, not drinking, not swearing, and not fooling around with girls. I knew that "the world" was a place of temptation: hard drinking, evil music, dirty jokes, and promiscuous sex. Outside the doors of the church, out there in the world, the devil "roamed to and fro," threatening everything I held to be true and good, and I needed to be constantly on guard lest I stumble and end up a backsliding believer.

I went to the same school from kindergarten through grade twelve, and I never felt any good reasons to question my teachers' authority. My idea of a rational world was shaped by my school principal, who also taught high school math. His years in the military gave him a confidence and authority that was often terrifying—he could be as intimidating as an army drill sergeant, and when he got angry, the sound of his voice always gave me shivers. I never ended up on his bad side (in part because I always worked hard in school, and because my dad was on the school board) and I thought he was brilliant and that his knowledge of history, math, science, and politics was nearly perfect. He taught with unwavering confidence, and he routinely preached about the precision and infallibility of math and science. He taught us that the world is logical, rational, orderly, and precise, which seemed to mesh seamlessly with my understanding of Christianity. I trusted that God, too, was logical, rational, orderly, and precise, just like the world he had made.

I went to Bible college straight out of high school. I figured I would eventually go to university to study something in math or science—maybe engineering or astronomy—but I wanted two years of Bible school under my belt to bolster my faith for all the big spiritual challenges I would have to face. I figured that my youth group friends who went straight into their secular university education were naïve and probably didn't really take their faith all that seriously. I imagined university would be a tidal wave of new ideas, most of which I expected to be fundamentally contrary to my Christian faith, and I wanted to be spiritually prepared to navigate my way through the world of dangerous, threatening ideas without losing my faith.

Bible college wasn't anything like the five-days-a-week Sunday school lesson I was expecting. I had to study harder than I ever had before, read more in a single semester than I'd read in all of high school, and plow through books that I didn't really understand at all, but the academic stress was outweighed by the adventure of being away from home and living in dorm (which felt like being in a giant camp cabin) and the sheer bliss of falling in love with Erika.

The first year of school warmed me up for year two, when big ideas started to work their way into my head and raze the foundations upon which I'd based my entire system of beliefs. I remember the feel of the unspectacular morning two weeks into the semester when everything began to change: the sound of the desks and chairs in that second-floor classroom, the early-fall sunlight, the students around me, the face and gentle voice of the sessional lecturer who drove out from Winnipeg to teach "The Education Program of The Church." There was nothing particularly earth shattering about the moment, nor about the lecture itself—something to do with the psychological and developmental aspects of Christian education—but for the first time in my life, something he said caused me to take a quick glance at my faith from an outside point of view.

Until that moment I had always assumed that the worldview I had inherited was basically self-evident, that any thinking person would see the strength and logic of the conservative, evangelical perspective I held as my own. I knew who God was and how he worked and what he expected of me. I had Jesus in my heart, which meant that I was a true Christian, and I believed that my life of faith from the day when I first said that prayer of salvation was about doing more good things and less bad things. My view from inside faith offered me an explanation for everything, from the origins of the cosmos to the faintest ripple in my conscience, and everything that was in between.

It had never seriously occurred to me that there were other legitimate ways to look at Christian belief, but here I was, sitting in a classroom in a conservative evangelical Bible college listening to this teacher, a committed Christian and a pastor of a church, offer a secular, non-spiritual, psychological explanation for something that I was sure was all about God. Something in my mind started to crack, just a thin fracture, too small to seem really significant, but serious enough that I still remember it sixteen years later. It wasn't doubt—that would come later, and with such unrelenting force that I was sure I was damned. This was something much more subtle, an experience of intellectual incongruity, an inability to make things fit where I thought they were supposed to. It was the first blow to my airtight view of the way things were, the beginning of a terrifying loss of certainty.

Sociology was like a sledgehammer driving a cold chisel into that intellectual and spiritual fracture, but at least sociology gave me terms like "anomie," and "paradigm shift" to describe what was happening to me, only it was more like a paradigm *loss* than a shift. I felt like I was falling out of belief into an empty, bottomless abyss. Learning to take a step back and look at religion and society as social phenomenon, as socially constructed reality and not self-evident reality made everything that I had considered fundamentally meaningful suddenly seem shallow and arbitrary. When I or anyone else uttered the word "God," did it actually have anything to do with God himself? Was my sensitive conscience simply a matter of social conditioning, and not the Holy Spirit convicting me? What did "faith" truly mean, and how could I continue to speak about "having faith" when I wasn't sure how to believe in anything? Was my personal walk with God more of an inheritance from the family, community, and tradition I grew up in than about who God actually was? How could I rely on language, so flimsy and malleable, so obviously itself a socially constructed reality, to convey any genuine meaning whatsoever? Could anyone truly say anything at all?

Sliding out of a random assortment of assumptions about "the human condition," what it means to be, in the words of Walker Percy, "lost in the cosmos," carries only a fraction of the existential burden of losing an all-encompassing worldview. The story I thought was mine purported to explain *everything*, but now I wasn't sure I could trust it to explain *anything*. Big questions came in thundering waves, following one on top of the other more quickly than I could sort them out. Learning was like an intellectual wrecking ball, knocking the foundations out from under everything that I believed. Thoughts and ideas chased one another through my head, one after the other, and the void they left became a hollow space for thin hopes to chase each other and disappear into black mist. By the time I reached midterms, I felt like I was losing my mind. The bottom was knocked out of everything I was used to standing on. Everything seemed tenuous. "Reality," I thought, was a thin veneer over a world of meaningless chaos. The night before I flew home for Thanksgiving I lay on my bed, unable to sleep, my thoughts running out of control. I was more anxious than I'd ever been in my life, and I was confident that this must be what it felt like to go mad.

For years to come, that same sense of madness would come over me now and then for no reason I could discern. I got a job working at a feed mill, and hit such a dark spell one morning that I climbed up on a big storage tank and wrote, "I AM LOSING MY MIND," with a fat Jiffy marker on a wall that no one would ever see. Another time I woke up in the middle of the night, sweating and terrified and full of nebulous dread, and I called my dad at three in the morning to ask him to pray for me. I remember working alongside a close friend one summer, when in the middle of our perfectly normal conversation, I became overpoweringly self-conscious about whatever I was saying. Mid-sentence, I suddenly lost all belief in words, and doubted that anything I could say would cross the gap between us. Whatever thoughts I had at that moment were completely gone, like a train roaring over a cliff, then nothing. Just silence, a blank, embarrassed look on my face, and my friend saying, "What the hell is the matter with you?" I felt like the priest in the movie *Big Bad Love*, during the scene when he presides over the funeral of a child:

> She shall suffer no more bla, bla. Platitude about the mysterious ways in which God works, about faith, platitude. Cliché, about God calling his children home, cliché, about angels, bla, bla. She shall suffer no more, bla. In the twinkling of an eye, bla. When the trumpet shall sound, bla, bla. And the dead shall be raised, incorruptible, bla, bla, bla. And we shall be changed.[1]

Those moments, when words would seem to fall and blow along like puffs of dust on a sidewalk, made me despise anyone who

1. Howard, *Big Bad Love*.

thought that something so simple and weak as flimsy verbs and fragile nouns could possibly communicate meaning. Part of me hated writers, philosophers, poets, storytellers, and most of all, preachers, for presumptuously playing with words, because when my all-powerful belief disappeared, I was left with a total void of meaning, and the only response I could see to such overwhelming meaninglessness was the silence of despair.

The poet and undertaker, Thomas Lynch, says, "The life of faith is less a journey into ever-more pleasant horizons or agreeable truths, and more a kind of rummage through the doubts raised by mere existence."[2] A faith crisis at eighteen is not all that special; it means it's time to grow up. I've learned to live with paradox, mystery, uncertainty, and doubt, and I have never regained that sense of confidence or security I used to know so well. But I have not completely let go of that longing for the orderly precision of certainty.

A day at home—wake up the kids, get them dressed, make breakfast, clean up, get to school, do chores, make lunch, clean up again, more chores, walk to school again, make a snack, start supper, clean up again, supervise some playtime, break up fights, bathe them, brush their teeth, and tuck them into bed—or a day at work—give my best to my job and then come home to a household that needs more than I feel I have to give—can weigh on me with dread that makes me tremble, and the feelings of madness and meaninglessness start to creep up again. I remember the stories a long-time friend of mine wrote around the time of his divorce, how he sat slouched in his living room chair, sucking a brown bottle and sneering as his wife cried tearful accusations while packing up a suitcase of clothes to move back home with her parents. I think of the stereotypes of the impossibly matched husband and wife, living out their dead lives joined only by a mortgage and the genes they contributed to their disappointed, disappointing offspring, bound by resentment, no longer engaged enough to be combative, resigned to perfect politeness. Even the word "love" starts to feel like dust, meaningless and empty.

I have to push myself to sit down here to try to turn these thoughts and feelings and memories about marriage into words because I tremble at

2. Lynch, *Booking Passage*, 151.

the work, walking a fine line between meaning and nothingness. Have I arrived at "mystery" for my explanation again? When the fear, doubt, and despair wash over me, rather than nurture the gifts of language and love, I feel tempted to smash them, or abandon them, because they can never be as solid as I think I need them to be.

"Marriage is mystery; words are mystery:" it feels like a cheap excuse for an answer, but it's the nearest thing I can find for an explanation. I cannot find absolutes or certainty in them, and I get no closer to what I sometimes think I am looking for by working harder and harder at it. Writing is always one step removed from reality; I trust that meaning is greater than the words I struggle to find to make sense of it. Love is as much an act of faith as faith itself. Love will never replace the certainty I used to have; even so, I trust that it is more than base biological instinct.

I go to church every week and I recite the creeds alongside my brothers and sisters, but deep down, I know that Christian hope is preposterous. In the face of all the real, tangible problems of the world, we Christians gather together and participate in a simple ritual with a cup of wine and a loaf of bread: that is our response. In the face of tyranny, tragedy, disaster, war, violence, greed, lust, vengeance, envy, and pride, the Eucharist is our act of resistance. This is what we offer to the world. This is our hope, our revolution. Fragile, small, ridiculous, staking it all on our trust in the crucified God, executed for sedition, dying the common death of a disgraced criminal. That is God's response to the world. Writing about the Gospel of Mark, Eugene Peterson says that the entire second half of the book focuses on death talk. "That doesn't sound very promising, especially for those of us who are looking for a text by which to live, a text by which to nurture our souls. But there it is."[3]

There it is.

Holding on to faith in the face of chaos. Writing in the face of meaninglessness. Staying with Erika when I'm scared as hell.

There it is. There she is, Erika, my wife. Here I am, filling a blank page with words, and there you are reading about it.

All of it—love, faith, hope, meaning, as fragile as ever.

I will not give in to despair.

3. Peterson, "Saint Mark: The Basic Text for Christian Spirituality," 8.

Let

All Striving

Cease

Our first home was a huge suite in a hundred-year-old apartment building in downtown Winnipeg. The clunking, hissing steam radiators would turn on and off randomly, sometimes not at all on cold days, and other times they would pump out so much heat that we had to open the balcony doors to balance the stifling temperature with a blast of Winnipeg winter. All the floors were original hardwood, scratched and scuffed, and they creaked nearly everywhere we walked, as did the floor in the suite above ours. The living room walls were covered in a century's layers of paint and wallpaper. In some places, when you got up close enough, you could make out the designs of gaudy, textured wallpaper that was probably fashionable fifty years ago. The high ceilings still had original light fixtures, and the bathroom had a big claw-foot tub and no shower. It was huge and beautiful, and the rent was very cheap. We had no furniture when we moved in, which made it all seem even bigger.

Early in our first winter, a couple months after our wedding, I stayed up late one night, reading a mystery novel about a translator whose brother mysteriously vanishes. It wasn't a particularly frightening story, but there was something about the night that made me feel anxious and afraid. Now, I have always been afraid of the dark. When I was young, I slept facing the door because I was afraid something might come to get me, and I wanted to be sure I could see it coming. After seeing a trailer for a scary-looking movie, *Cameron's Closet*, I always made sure to keep my closet door closed at night. Often I had horrific nightmares—cracked, bleeding photographs, ritualistic sacrifices behind our house, dancing devils tormenting my family—and when I woke up I had to turn on the lights in the hallway outside my door before I could fall asleep again.

So I kept reading, hoping that the tension in the story might resolve itself and help me feel better, but I started to imagine that there were eyes in the living room clock and ghostly hands behind the door. I was afraid to look out the window because I imagined seeing a reflection of something or someone sneaking up behind me. The little circle of light under the lamp where I was reading felt like the only safe place in the room. I was afraid to move, afraid of everything around me, of all the darkness waiting to get me.

When it was obvious that things were not going to get any better, I turned off the lamp and walked through the darkness to our bedroom where Erika had been sleeping for hours. Waking her up, I explained that I might be having an anxiety attack, something that had only happened once before, back in university, during midterms. "I'm all caught up in this feeling of darkness," I told her, "with horrible images swirling around in my head. There's something evil in the shadows, but it's inside me too."

Erika listened to me, held me and prayed for me, and as she prayed I had a waking dream that only lasted a few seconds. Standing at the top of a giant spiral staircase filled with brightly coloured shapes, I knew I was looking at a display of all my sins. As I started down the steps, I was sinking lower and lower, and I wondered where this journey was leading, if it would ever end, or if it was a voyage into hell. But I reached the bottom, which was like a cellar, and I saw the silhouette of someone standing there, and I heard a voice say, "Let all striving cease." The fear that had been building for hours disappeared. Erika prayed for me again, and within a couple minutes we both fell asleep and didn't wake up until late the next morning.

In the years since, I have thought about that night many times, struggling to accept this spiritual vision that seems like a divine invitation, though not as clear as the biblical accounts of visions so familiar to me. On the run from Esau, Jacob stopped for a night's sleep in the wilderness, used a rock for a pillow and dreamed of a ladder running all the way to heaven, with angels moving up and down the steps. When he woke, he said, "How awesome is this place!" and named it Bethel, meaning "House of God." The prophet Amos saw everyday kinds of items—locusts, fire, a plumb line, and a basket of fruit—each with a message of coming judgment. Ezekiel stood in the middle of a valley of bones and had a conversation with God as God pulled the bones together into skeletons, covered them flesh and set them marching like an army of zombies.[1]

But *Let all striving cease*? My ongoing response is like that of the man who asks Jesus to heal his demon-possessed son: "I do believe; help me overcome my unbelief!"[2] I believe, and I *want* to believe, but each morning as I listen to the news, nearly every story a reminder that evil is everywhere, the Christian story seems too good to be true. I still feel a kinship with those very things I despise. Like the man T Bone Burnett pursues in his song "Criminals:" the dangerous offender I'm after is the one under my own hat. Surely I need to pay for my sins, and suffer for my malicious, selfish, proud ways, because this is how things are supposed to work in the world. If I really am forgiven, I must first pay for what I've done. When I see grace, running like an untamed horse, I want to harness it and domesticate it, make it more reasonable, because somehow I still believe that if I strive a little bit harder, my life will turn out well. I'm still trying like hell to be good enough for heaven because grace and salvation seem too good to be true.

But this vision burns up my expectations about what I owe God and what I can expect from him, and the foolishness and excess of God's love has started to make more sense in light of the undeserved love Erika gives. It shines into my life, driving away the shadows in the dark rooms filled with shame, guilt, fear, and self-hatred. Brought into the light of love, my burdens disappear like fog, illuminating my gifts and strengths, hidden treasures I have not recognized, and bringing me back to life. *Let all striving cease.*

1. Genesis 28:10–19; Amos 7–8; Ezekiel 37:1–14.
2. Mark 9:24.

Even still, I want to tally the score, hedge my bets and keep my distance. I'm afraid to get too close. All my maladies, old wounds, the long-borne sin-sick ways of behaving that I have grown comfortable with keep hanging on, like pests I share my crumbs with when I know, instead, I should be trying to poison them. What if I let go of who I know myself to be, this settled comfort of second best? I am afraid of the risk of goodness. "If I meet God," asks Annie Dillard, "will he take and hold my bare hand in his, and focus his eye on my palm, and kindle that spot and let me burn?"[3]

But love is relentless in its effort to free me and heal me of my self-loathing and fear. Every day, in the minutiae of thousands of days spent with one another, or in the crises that roil and smash against us, I struggle to choose to open my palm to this burning gaze of love, endure the pain of healing.

Love, catch and consume my fear. *Help me overcome my unbelief!*

3. Dillard, "God in the Doorway," 139.

PART
FOUR

Love Is A Home

The Geology

of a

Young Marriage

sedimentary: of or relating to rocks formed by the deposition of sediment, solid fragments of rock or mineral that are carried and deposited by water, wind, or ice.

metamorphic: <u>changed</u> in structure as a result of metamorphism, the process by which rocks are altered in texture or internal structure by <u>extreme heat and pressure.</u>

The autumn after I graduated from high school, I packed everything I owned into my car and drove to a small town in southern Manitoba for Bible school. Four days into my freshman year, I noticed Erika, right about the time she noticed me. We tried to be casual about getting to know one another, but we hit it off quickly, and despite our efforts to avoid labels, we were one of the first freshman couples. I don't remember much from any of my classes that year: Erika had most of my attention. We were young—I was seventeen, she was nineteen—and maybe it was because we were young that <u>we so freely opened up the deepest places of our hearts and fell in love.</u>

Everything about those progressive early stages of romantic love was intoxicating; I can still recall bits when I watch my friends fall in love. Seeing them brings back some of the feelings from those early weeks and months with Erika. I remember how I tried to seem casual while aching to "accidentally" end up at a table close to hers in the dining room or the seat next to her in the lecture hall. I remember how my stomach would twist when I held her gaze for just a fraction of a second longer than the unspoken rules allow for mere friends. I remember the deep, warm satisfaction of our talks, all the time we spent together, sharing as much as we could about our histories, secrets, the plans and hopes and fears of what was to come. I remember the thrill of attraction to her body, as powerful as gravity, the first touches, the unforgettable first kiss—such holy beauty in all of these innocent firsts! And day by day, bit by bit, each sweet moment between us was gradually making the two of us one, our separate lives winding together to create one story, like layer upon layer, slowly shaping us into husband and wife.

Oh, I remember that irreplaceable sweetness of young love.

Limestone is a sedimentary rock made from the compressed shells of crustaceans—ancient coral reefs, clams, and snails. In certain aquatic zones these shells pile up into layers and layers of shells and over time, the accumulated pressure of these shells and the ocean pressing down on them can create limestone. It becomes usable when the sea dries up or recedes far enough to allow some builder access to it.

The Manitoba Legislature in Winnipeg is about a five-minute walk from my house, and it is certainly the grandest limestone building in the city. The stone comes from a Tyndall stone quarry at Garson, twenty kilometers northeast of the city, an area which was once the floor of the prehistoric *Lake Aggasiz*. The limestone is prized for its light color and the fossils of sea creatures still visible in the cut stone. My family took a tour of the building, and our guide pointed out some of most notable fossils in the walls. The Legislature is a towering landmark, with its arches and columns, overlooking the Assiniboine River, just upstream from the historically rich Forks, where the Assiniboine and Red Rivers meet. Erika and I got married in a limestone church, and our wedding pictures were at the Legislature. Sometimes I bike around the grounds with my kids, and I always tell them stories about our wedding day, about how it snowed and about how beautiful their mama was.

After more than ten years of marriage, our days of newlywed bliss are long behind us. We had our round of the beautiful firsts while falling in love in Bible college, then a second round of "firsts" when we got back together after having spent years apart, and finally plunged naively and blissfully into all the ecstatic firsts of married life. But our drawn-out honeymoon phase eventually ended. Though there are still new things in store for us, what once seemed like an endless crescendo of romantic ecstasy reached its peak a long time ago, and now most of married life is unspectacular. The highs and lows and the give-and-take of love have become more familiar and routine.

Which is a problem for me. All my life I have been idealistic and sentimental. I love to savor the things I know are good, and sometimes it is hard for me not to wish we could go back to all those firsts in the early stages of my life with Erika. I feel it most intensely when I see my close friends fall in love. I recognize the bliss of being in love, and it reminds me that Erika and I have long since passed through our romantic innocence. The memories of those times are still sweet, but sometimes I find it hard to accept that, for Erika and I, those days are gone.

I tell myself that *surely* there is much more to love than cheesy romance. Surely the strength and longevity of marriage does not depend on the ecstasy of those feelings. Anyone who tries to hold onto that feeling of being desperately in love is living a dream from which they will inevitably experience a rude awakening. Romantic love looks like that in the movies, but the revolving door of the typical Hollywood movie star marriage is a sure sign that that kind of love is only temporary.

But I can't quite let go of the romantic longings. I am sometimes still seduced by the powerful myth of the singular desirability of young, romantic love. My desire is, at least in part, fostered by consumer culture where at every turn we are promised that ultimate satisfaction can be found by leaving behind whatever you have now and moving on to something new. Whether that's a new laundry soap, makeup, automobile or lover, it doesn't matter. There's no need to let something old and worn out—read: familiar, routine, everyday—come between us and the happiness we deserve. It is a powerful, ubiquitous message, one that I struggle to resist but am still tempted by. In the face of these seductive promises, what am I to make of this vow of lifelong commitment to just one person, to Erika? What if *they* are right? What if romantic love is true love, and when the romance fades, love is gone? What good is there in staying together when the sweet, easy fun of falling in love is gone? What good are loyalty and fidelity without the ecstasy of first love?

Marble is a metamorphic rock that comes from limestone. Under the same sorts of conditions that turn coal into diamonds—intense heat and pressure over a long period of time—limestone changes into marble. Marble is an exquisite building material, more rare than limestone and much more costly. Its unique physical and aesthetic properties set it apart from other types of building stones. Whereas a stone like quartz is a crystal and can only be cut according to the cleavage lines of the crystal, marble's beauty is comparable to a crystal, but it can be carved rather than simply cut as with crystalline minerals. Throughout the process of metamorphosis, the impurities of the limestone become concentrated, creating distinct colors and lines in the marble. The Manitoba Legislature has grand, polished white marble floors streaked with seams of grey, brown, and black, making every square inch of it distinct and unique. Erika and I had our wedding pictures taken there, and in one of them you can see Erika's reflection in the floor, like she's standing by water.

The beautiful, strong "marble" of married love starts with the layers of young love, but over time it becomes something else, something stronger. Limestone is soft; it can be crushed into powder. Marble is more resilient. I can see the prized, costly marble of love beginning to form in my marriage, and when I recognize it for what it is, I know that it's fine to let go of my young, romantic love, because that stage is over and past. Now Erika and I must move from the passive gravity of young love to the more challenging work of keeping this love strong through the ongoing heat and pressure of everyday life.

I'm not trying to disparage the beauty of young love to try to make myself feel superior, but I need to remind myself that it is as fleeting as it is common. It is not better than this older, less spectacular love; it is something different. This love between Erika and I is becoming stronger and more complex, less prone to being chipped than our young love was, yet it still needs to be protected and cared for. It doesn't necessarily draw immediate attention to itself, because its beauty is in the inch-by-inch details gradually becoming visible after years of transformation. Love that is like marble is rare and precious; the heat and pressure of life crush many attempts at love into dust. But for those who are willing, those who wait with patience and hope for love's metamorphosis, they will find it is much stronger and more valuable than they ever could have known otherwise.

Love

Is

a Home[1]

CHAPTER

16

I've been thinking a lot about place, about the ways that the place a person comes from becomes a part of who they are. It's heavy these days because I have recently left behind a place that had become home, and moved to a place that is new and unfamiliar, where I still feel more like a tourist than a resident. Just before Christmas, I got together with Brick for lunch, and we talked about the farming community in southern Alberta where we both grew up, and about the different places we had visited and lived in since we moved away from home. Brick has traveled a lot. His work keeps him busy and often away from home, and he has adapted to it very well. But despite his smooth, cosmopolitan urban style and his ability to thrive in the mazes of some of the world's busiest cities, the ways of small town life have marked him indelibly.

When I was a kid, I was always impressed and more than just a little intimidated by how hard a worker Brick was. All of the practical characteristics that farming requires—commitment, neighborliness, generosity, hard-

1. This chapter comes from a speech I gave at Brick Blair and Marianne Corless' wedding in May, 2004.

nosed realism, tenacity—these things shaped Brick, and in whatever he has done since leaving home, he has always worked like a farmer. He still bears many of the gifts and burdens of his hometown, the inheritances of farming and rural life. He knows the satisfactions of hard work through the passing of the seasons, the risks, faith, doubts, and losses inherent in daily living, the give-and-take nature of work. He carries with him the knowledge of our inescapable dependence on circumstances and factors beyond our control. It goes without saying that Brick would not be the man he is today had he grown up somewhere other than on Crocus Plains Ranch, twelve miles southeast of Youngstown.

But at the same time, and for as long as I have known him, Brick has lived in between the competing demands and interests of vastly different worlds, in an uncomfortable sort of liminal space. At least part of the reason that I have always admired him so much is that we both share a sort of restlessness that comes from living in one place, yet feeling drawn to other, unknown places. Brick could always work just as hard as any of his farming peers, but he also loved to play sad songs on his guitar, write poetry, read obscure books for enjoyment, fix up old, abandoned cars—all sorts of highly impractical interests. No doubt there were plenty of others in our community who were similarly restless with farming life, but I don't remember anyone other than Brick who was exploring so many interests outside of what his immediate surroundings had to offer. He worked just as hard at playing his guitar or writing poems as he did when he was shovelling barley or feeding the cows.

I know that the different directions each one of us take in our lives are rarely based upon clear and distinct either/or kinds of decisions. All of us live with a sense that we are not entirely comfortable in our own place, and most of us choose how to live by balancing what we know well and are most familiar with, against the uncomfortable restlessness that keeps us moving, keeps us interested in trying something new and just a little bit threatening. But Brick had that restlessness more than most. He's been away from the farm for a long time now. He has left the life of a farmer for that of the jet-setting urban dweller. But he has continued to exist in liminal space, somewhere in between hard-nosed practicality and the dreams of making impractical, beautiful things.

Eventually his restlessness led him back to school, and when he went to university, he discovered a rich atmosphere full of things that were new and exciting, new ways of thinking and looking at the world, libraries full of surprising, challenging books, communities of artists, writers and thinkers. The atmosphere of ideas at university can be overwhelming at first, but at the same time it can be completely exhilarating, and Brick thrived in it all. Yet he was probably no less in between than when he was on the farm. Living in the city, and holed up in the often self-indulgent, self-important atmosphere of the academy, Brick soaked up all the ideas his cosmopolitan professors had to offer him, and then wrote about the life he knew best, stories about working on the farm and about life with neighbors, and he wrote poems and songs about rusted out pickup trucks, rodeos, drunks, horses, combines, and dusty back roads at sunset.

As much as he succeeded in school, he never entirely trusted in it. He never talked himself into believing that academia was a place he could call home. By now, for sure, he had discovered too many interesting things for it to be possible for him to ever fit neatly back into the life and faith of his roots, but at the same time he was marked enough by his years of sweat and grease and dust to ever be convinced that the intellectuals could give him everything he was looking for, or tell him the answers to all the things he wanted most of all to know.

In between.

At the heart of all of my lasting, trusted friendships is the sense that in all the struggles and complexities and joys of life, we are somehow in this together. Part of the reason why now, after many years apart and only occasional conversations, I still think of Brick as a good friend is that I, like him, feel pulled between the demands and interests of two very different worlds. I know the burning wonder that learning can inspire, the deep satisfaction of reading, the thrill of becoming carried away in a passionate, intellectual conversation, the joy of knowing that there is still so much out there that I do not know. These pleasures of learning are very real; I love them, and my appetite for learning seems to be always increasing. I worry sometimes that I won't have enough time for all the things I want to do. I've got a holy, restless longing that keeps me active and alive and eager to keep learning as much as I can.

But at the same time, I know what it is to be rooted in a place. I long very much for that—to learn the kinds of lessons about life that can only come by staying committed to one place for twenty, thirty, forty years. I am really not much more than a small town boy with a pragmatic, farmer-like view of the world. I've spent many years in school, but I can never really believe in academics either, or put my faith in scholarship the way some people seem to be able to. I cannot, in all honesty, convert. When I find myself surrounded by intellectual, bookish types who think the world is mainly about abstract ideas, and who think that milk comes from a carton and not a cow, I feel out of place. I miss the farm. I can talk along for a while, play the same sort of heady games that they do, but eventually I get tired of it, or I lose track of what they're saying. Eventually it all starts to seem like nonsense, or like some contest of confusing words and abstract philosophies. I'll drop in a comment about tractors or cowshit, just to try to dumb things down a bit and bring us all back to reality, something to get our feet back on the ground.

I can play both sides. By now, I have far too many questions and interests to ever really fit comfortably back into the good little small town churchboy role I used to play, but at the same time I have too much faith and have seen too much of what seems like God's goodness to go along with the philosophical types who, in the end, want me to trust them when they say that they have come to the conclusion we're all alone in the universe. I can play both games, but I am at home in neither world.

Something new has happened to me though, and it is something that I see happening in Brick: it's the fresh, life-giving, unpredictable process wrought by love. It's the kind of love that's like a sort of homecoming, like finding something that you didn't even know you'd lost. It's that spark of recognition in the face of someone you've only just met, and it brings with it an unmistakable peace. It's more than a distraction from the restlessness, or something to temporarily numb the restless feelings; it's a true peace, the peace of a home. In only a few years of being married to Erika, I have found the peace that has begun to displace my anxious restlessness. Erika has become my home. It's not an answer to the question of where to live, but it gives my heart a place to be, regardless of where we live. In the few times that I've seen Brick and Marianne together, it seems to me that love has made a place for Brick to be at home, no longer just in between. And that is a remarkable gift. Not everyone finds that sort of love, but I wish that everyone would. I am grateful to have found a home in love, and I celebrate every time someone else finds something of the same.

Love leaves its mark upon your heart and your life, whether you want it to or not. It's painful and difficult, and as far as I can tell, it's still the only thing worth living for. The making and the unmaking that love performs is both a sowing and an uprooting. Love is part sledge-hammer and part scalpel. It is the wounding and the healing, like a painful journey into wholeness and life more abundant. It's stronger, more surprising, and more challenging than one could ever imagine. It's not safe, but it is good.)cs Lewis

The things I am discovering, trying to put into words, are not new, and Brick and Marianne have known this love for a long time. But a wedding like this is a fitting way to celebrate the sort of love that becomes a home for us, love that continuously invites us into the wide circle of goodness that comes down from above and lifts us up, like grace.

Blessings to you both.

Locust Years

CHAPTER 17

In the most important sense, history is not an attempt to
record everything; it is a quest to discover, by means of
words and images, a shape in the course of time—to figure
the Why and How of events.

—Robert Farrar Capon,
Hunting the Divine Fox

After dating for just two years, Erika
and I broke up for a handful of very practical, sensible
reasons, and though we'd been apart more than twice
as long as we'd been together, I couldn't get over her.
Love or sentimental obsession—I couldn't tell the difference anymore—haunted me, and all my memories
of her survived every one of my attempts to let her go.

A good friend of mine set me up on a date with
someone she had known growing up and we spent a
couple months together, trying to build some kind of
relationship, but it was doomed from the start because
I couldn't stop comparing how I felt about her with
how I still felt for Erika, whom I hadn't spoken to in
years. I figured she was dating someone else, maybe

even married by now. I was haunted by her memory like she was a ghost, watching over the shoulder of every new romantic interest in case she would suddenly appear. The woman I was dating grew tired of sharing me with a memory, and we broke up. It wasn't the first time I had dated someone else, desperately hoping to find a strong enough connection to unwind the ways I felt tied to Erika, but it had never worked, and the end of this romance felt like the dead-end of my last hope. It sent me into a dark spiral of self-destructive thoughts.

I had some friends who knew me well and looked after me, neighbors from upstairs who cared for me like I was their son. Others that I had known for years sat patiently and listened as I rambled on to them, retelling such a familiar story to them by now. My mom flew out to spend a day with me when I was at my lowest. We sat out in the courtyard behind my apartment and talked late into the night. I smoked my pipe and tried to be honest without telling her everything. I didn't want her to worry about me. I wanted to make it seem like I was going to be okay because I didn't know how to tell her I was falling apart.

But I felt like I needed to get out of the city for a while, get away from my painful memories and my dead-ends and mistakes; a change of scenery. Dad offered me a couple months work on the farm, helping with harvest, so I packed my car with bags of clothes and CD's and books and drove from Winnipeg back to my parents farm just outside Youngstown, Alberta.

The twelve hours on the road gave me time to think about what it would be like to be back on the farm for more than the usual couple days' visit. When I was seventeen, I moved away from home because I knew I didn't want to be a farmer. I never loved farming life the way that so many of my friends seemed to, and by the time I finished high school I couldn't wait to get off the farm and out of the small town. Rural life seemed boring, small, narrow and uninteresting. I wanted culture and music and art, more diversity, a life of surprises and excitement. The little college where I first met Erika was just south of Winnipeg, and when I finished my degree I moved into the city to be with my friends and to live where the action was.

But now that I had lived in the city for a few years, it was starting to become clear to me just what I had left behind. City life had much of what I felt like I was looking for. It was rich and diverse and exciting, full of interesting events and people. But it made me feel very small. It was a place of anonymity and competitiveness, crowds, noise, and endless bustling. I was too restless to ever be entirely satisfied with rural life, but at the same time I didn't feel big enough for everything that the city had to offer. Spending time back home on the farm was something I looked forward to. It meant coming back to my past and to a kind of comfort in all the familiar things about it. Now that I was going to be home for a couple months, I realized how much I missed not just the slower, quieter pace of small town life, but the farm too, our farm: the crops that would be ripening, the wide acres of pasture and hayfields, the patches of trees, the hills and coulees, the abandoned homesteads we liked to explore when we were young, the grid of back roads and long, straight fences.

Dad sent me out on the tractor the day after I got home, and right away I started to fall in love with the things of farming life that I had tried to escape from. I loved the early morning start and the simplicity of driving the tractor around the field all day long. I loved the view out of the west-facing window of the kitchen where the prairie stretched out into a gradual hill that pushed the horizon out twenty miles. To the east were grain bins and a machine shed, and past that, wide fields of golden barley, oats and wheat, bushy crops of mustard, ready to be harvested, and hay fields full of bales and alfalfa and crested wheat. The sunsets were bright orange and red and pink and yellow, dusty and hazy. Sometimes in the evening I would drive down the back road to town and park at the top of the big hill, and I'd sit on the trunk of my car and smoke cigarettes, feeling sneaky and enjoying the sunset. It was a relief to have left behind the concrete and glass towers and ceaseless traffic of the city. Harvest was the busiest time of the year on the farm, but it was busyness with a story and purpose, unlike the rest-less, noisy scurrying of the city. The landscape, the roads, the fields, the neighbors and friends who stayed—it all felt meaningful, and it was all familiar. It felt just right to me, exactly what I was hoping for.

Dad and Mom didn't have anyone other than me helping with harvest. Usually they had a hired man who helped out all year long, and sometimes a second helper during harvest, but not that year. The summer had brought more rain than my dad could remember ever having seen before, and it had come at just the right times. My parents farmed in one of the driest areas on the prairies, famous for drought and grasshoppers and terrible dust storms. The farmers around there complained a lot because they were always desperate for rain, living like gamblers that had put their last bit of savings into some high-stakes roll. Things were always tight. But this year it finally looked different. This year, the crops looked promising—tall, thick, even, heads fat with grain, the kind of year my dad had been waiting for his whole life.

Since he was a kid, Dad had always been a farmer at heart, but the past ten years of farming had been getting more and more difficult for him. All his life he had battled a severe dust allergy and now that he was getting older his back was starting to give out on him. The costs of large-scale farming were always increasing but the crops never really seemed to do any better, and grain prices never seemed to rise enough to balance the escalating costs. Life-long grievances with people in the community and at church were starting to wear on him. But most of all—or maybe because of it all—Dad seemed to have lost the joy he had in farming. Every year it was becoming more stressful and less satisfying, and his heart just wasn't in it like it used to be.

So now the farm had been paid off for only about six years, but Dad and Mom already wanted to sell the place. They were considering an offer from a guy who lived a few hours north, an entrepreneur who had bought the farm south of ours and had hired somebody to move down and manage the place for him. Dad and Mom weren't enthusiastic about selling the place to some absentee landlord who would most likely plow everything under and turn the carefully tended landscape into a giant pasture, but they also knew it wasn't just anyone who could afford to walk in and buy a big farm like ours. If they didn't sell to him they might never be able to sell it at all, and they seemed anxious to move on to something else. If they accepted his offer, this would be their last year on the farm. It seemed fitting that it would be a bumper crop.

It felt good to be home helping out. Part of the reason I was never much in love with farming was because I was never much in love with the heat and long hours of sunshine in the summer. But autumn meant shorter, cooler days, which suited me fine. On the days that it rained, Dad and I would haul bales in from the hay fields or fix fences or work on small projects around the yard. If it was just a bit too cloudy and humid to harvest, we would bale hay or change cultivator shovels.

Sometimes dad would give me a couple days off, and I would go up to Edmonton to stay with my brother, or drive an hour and a half to Drumheller, home of the Royal Tyrrell Museum of Paleontology, not to go to the museum, but to shop at a fantastic little record store called T-Rex. Once Dad took me into Calgary to watch the stock car races at the speedway, and on the drive home that night we had our best ever father-son conversation, and afterwards I felt like I'd been waiting my whole life to talk to him like that.

But it was the harvest I enjoyed most. Harvest was the high point of the year, the culmination of months of work and worry and waiting, the big payoff. In spite of the anxiety every farmer felt about trying to get the crops in ahead of rain or frost or snow, there was always an air of excitement and a sense of accomplishment. Dad and I traded back and forth, one of us driving the combine while the other drove the grain truck on the field, and hauled the full loads back to the yard. The crops were just as good as Dad had guessed they would be, and it was always a bit of a race to try to get the full grain truck home, unloaded, and back to the field before the combine was full again and waiting to unload. We quit early one windless, clear evening, and Dad took me up in his little two-seater airplane, and I took some black and white photos of the patterns that our work had left on the fields. I snapped a quick shot of him as he looked out the front window and up at the clouds, and it's still one of my favorite pictures.

Mom made us lunches big enough to last for the day, full of fruit, fresh bread, and cookies. I usually ate everything before noon. Sometimes dad would drive into town to get a tire fixed or to pick up a part from the farm supply shop, and he'd come back with something more to eat. He would drive up close to the combine and motion for me to keep moving. He would jog to catch up and then climb up to the cab and deliver me a huge bag of chips and a liter of pop. "Just thought you might need a little snack," he'd say, matter of factly.

We were giddy over how great the crops were. He said that in all his years on the farm he couldn't remember ever seeing crops like this. He remembered harvests that had been a fifth this good, but he'd only ever dreamed of having a harvest like this. It was good for my soul to see Dad's excitement. At the end of every day he would thank me for my work, and tell me how glad he was that I was home to help out. He'd tell me, "I don't know how I would have managed to do it without you," and I always thought he would have figured out some way to get by, but it was still good to hear. I was just glad for the work, for the time at home, most of all for the escape from the city. I needed to be home as much as they needed me there.

But I couldn't leave everything behind. I was still myself: anxious, depressed, still stuck on Erika. I'd come home late after work and read or watch TV. I felt like Mom wanted to talk to me most evenings, maybe ask how I was doing, but I was never quite sure what I should tell her. I wanted to say that I was doing fine, but I still didn't really think that I was, so mostly I was just quiet. The long, solitary days driving the tractor gave me hours to brood over the things I had come home to try to forget, and before too long the same questions that had been my undoing when I was in Winnipeg rolled around inside my head as I drove circles around the fields. Erika was out of my life, but she was still in my heart—hopelessly sentimental but true. How was I going to reconcile my longing with her absence? Clearly I was not getting over her, but did I even want to let her go? Had I made her into my tragic story that I carried around with me, like an emotional show-and-tell? Was I just using her as an excuse to feel sorry for myself, or to get others to feel sorry for me? I had pined for her so intensely and for so long that I worried about what our relationship had really been like and what I was simply making up in retrospect. Was I remembering a love story that was sweeter than the actual love itself? Was I longing for her because I was selfish and simply couldn't let her go? The last time I had heard anything from her was by letter, more than a year ago, and the tone of it made me think that she was over me. Why couldn't I get over her? If I could see her again, maybe I could try to get some answers and find that elusive closure.

One afternoon I made a mental list of the friends that she and I had in common, wondering whether or not we might both be invited to the same wedding, and just accidentally bump into one another. The list was short. Some were already married, others had broken up and weren't likely to get back together just to provide me with the possibility of finding a bit of closure with an old love. So once more I gave up. I told myself I would probably never see her again, and I hoped that maybe this time, I could really let go of her.

Two days later, after we had serviced and fuelled up the combine, I had the grain truck ready to go to the field for the first load of the day.

I pulled around in front of the house and when I went inside to pick up the lunches for Dad and myself, Mom came down to meet me at the bottom of the stairs. She handed me the lunch boxes and then put her arm around my shoulder and said, "Guess who called?" She grinned.

Oh no, I thought, the ex-girlfriend.

"Erika," she said.

Erika. "Really?" I asked.

"Yes. She thought you were in Winnipeg and she was going there tonight. She wanted to take you out for supper, but she didn't know how to get in touch with you so she called here to get your number. I told her you would call her back tonight."

I thought, I should just get in my car right now and drive to Winnipeg, and I should go out for supper with her, just like she asked.

Instead, I thought about her all day, and then I called her that night when I was done with work. I turned off the living room lights and sat on the rocking chair in the dark, not knowing how this would go. I had so many tangled, confused knots of feelings and memories.

But we talked for two solid hours, awkward and nervous at the start, almost like strangers, then more freely, more from the soul than from nerves. Her voice was kind, just like I remembered it, and it soothed my nerves. I pictured her face and eyes and hands, and instead of trying to push those memories away I relished them. I felt like it was suddenly safe for me to remember her again. I felt the goodness of it right down to my bones.

After finishing with the harvest, I headed back to Winnipeg to start a job at a daycare. Erika was in Brandon, ten hours from the farm and two hours from Winnipeg. In our years apart, I had to drive past Brandon every time I went home, and I felt a gnawing ache every single time I approached the city, but this time it was different. She'd asked me to meet her for supper, and she'd had to wait a month, but now I was taking her up on the invitation.

I could feel the excitement tingling all the way to the tips of my thumbs when I turned off the highway into the city, and I followed the instructions she had given me—East entrance, over the train tracks, behind the hospital. I parked in the visitor's lot in front of the brown brick nurse's residence. I sat outside for a second in the dark, trying to drink in the moment. Another nurse was leaving the building as I was walking up, and he let me in the door behind him. Instead of taking the elevator, I climbed the three flights of stairs to her floor. I had waited for so long for this, and now I wanted to take my time, to savor the satisfaction of our reunion.

I needed years, not minutes, years to believe that she was really back, years to soak up all that it meant to have her back in my life. (It still makes me tremble. More than a decade after that day I still look at her sometimes and find it hard to believe that she's back, she's really back. It's Erika. I've loved her so long.) When I got to her room, her door was halfway open. She was lying on her stomach on her bed, reading. That was how she always read when she was studying to be a nurse.

I stepped back for a second. Not out of fear, really, but because this was what I had been dreaming of for so long. It was like so many things had fallen together and brought me here to her again.

Then I knocked on the door and went in. She got up and walked slowly to me and hugged me, and the fit of her body against me and her arms around me was exactly the way that I had remembered it.

She fit perfectly.

Later over supper, I said to her, "I want to be with you again, but I feel like I need some time so sort out some of my problems first." She said that was fine with her. She knew that I was back, and that was enough for her.

Months later she would tell me that she had decided to call me out of the blue because she was tired of wondering where I was and what I was doing and if I still loved her. She didn't know whether or not I even lived in the country, or if I was already married, but after nearly five years of wondering and longing, she had had enough: she called me up because she wanted to marry me.

And one year later, she did.

Works Cited

Abbey, Edward. "Watching the Birds: The Windhover." In *Down The River*, 49–55. New York: Dutton, 1982.

Berry, Wendell. "Goods." In *Collected Poems: 1957–1982*, 200. New York: Counterpoint, 1985.

———. *Life Is A Miracle*. Washington: Counterpoint, 2001.

———. "Marriage." In *Collected Poems: 1957–1982*, 70. New York: Counterpoint, 1985.

———. "Poetry and Marriage." In *Standing By Words*, 92–105. Washington: Shoemaker and Hoard, 2005.

———. "Sex, Economy, Freedom and Community." In *Sex, Economy, Freedom and Community*, 117–73. New York: Pantheon, 1992.

Bolt, Robert. *A Man For All Seasons*. Agincourt: Bellhaven House, 1974.

Cairns, Scott. "Loves." In *Philokalia*, 159–62. Lincoln: Zoo Press, 2002.

Capon, Robert Farrar. "An Offering Of Uncles." In *The Romance of The Word*, 35–166. Grand Rapids: Wm. B. Eerdmans, 1995.

Chesterton, G. K. *Orthodoxy*. Mineola, NY: Dover, 2004; New York: Dodd, Mead & Company, 1908.

———. *The Man Who Was Thursday*. Ware: Wordsworth Editions, 1995.

Dillard, Annie. "God in the Doorway." In *Teaching a Stone to Talk*, 137–39. New York: Harper Perennial, 1982.

Frangione, Lucia. *Espresso*. Vancouver: Talonbooks, 2004.

Gunton, Colin. *The One, The Three, and The Many*. Cambridge: Cambridge University Press, 1993.

Hoskyns, Barney. *Lowside Of The Road*. New York: Broadway Books, 2009.

Lynch, Thomas. "Fish Stories." In *Bodies in Motion and At Rest*, 151–57. New York: Norton, 2000.

———. *Booking Passage*. New York: W.W. Norton, 2005.

Mason, Mike. *The Mystery of Marriage*. Portland: Multnomah, 1985.

Peterson, Eugene. "Saint Mark: The Basic Text for Christian Spirituality." In *Subversive Spirituality*, 3–15. Vancouver: Regent College Publishing, 1997; Grand Rapids: Eerdmans, 1994.

Polanyi, Michael. *The Tacit Dimension*.

Robinson, Marilynne. "Psalm Eight." In *The Death of Adam*, 227–44. New York: Picador, 1998, 2005.

Schoemer, Karen. "More Dylan than Dylan," *Newsweek*. (May 10, 1999). No pages. Online: http://www.newsweek.com/id/88269

Taylor, Terry Scott. "What I Should Have Said." From *Avocado Faultline*. Silent Planet Records, 2000.

Waits, Tom. "Better Off Without A Wife." From *Nighthawks at the Diner*. Asylum Records, 1975.

———. "Emotional Weather Report." From *Nighthawks at the Diner*. Asylum Records, 1975.

———. "Take It With Me." From *Mule Variations*. Anti, 1999.

Acknowledgments

Thanks to Kyle and Stephanie Armstrong, Ron and Karin Armstrong, Shawn Barber, Don Betts, Evan Braun, Will Braun and Jennifer de-Groot, Aiden Enns and Karen Schlichting, Sharon Gallagher, Jason Goode, Christopher Holmes, David Jacobsen, Doug Koop, Kent and Dee Kroeker, Walter and Anne Kruse, Stuart McLean and Jess Milton, Miriam Meinders, Kevin Nikkel, Geoff Penner, and the staff at JJ Bean, Main Street, Vancouver, BC.

Thanks to the many friends at Grandview Calvary Baptist Church in Vancouver, BC, who helped nurture the first stage of this book, and to the now far-flung writers and artists and thinkers who shaped me and this book: Kirsten Behe, Annie (Lam) Day, Tim Dickau, Dave Diewert, Stephen Hitchcock, Eddy Hopkins, Susan Kennedy, Peter LaGrand, Matt Malyon, Ruth (Tank) Pswazro, Charles Ringma, Dal Schindel, Andy Shaver, Emily Stassen, Steve Stasson, Andrew Thistlethwaite, Katy Wehr, and Loren and Mary Ruth Wilkinson.

Thanks to Rob and Colleen Kwade, for friendship and for their heroic, saving efforts.

Deep, ongoing thanks to the parish of St. Margaret's Anglican Church, Winnipeg, who supported me with generosity, patience, and encouragement.

Thanks to the Manitoba Arts Council for generous financial support.

Thank you, Maxine Hancock, for encouragement and guidance.

Thank you, Karen Hollenbeck Wuest, for the hours of loving, skilful, and precise editing.

Thank you, Christian Amondson, for championing this for me. God bless you, my friend.

Thank you, Molly and Jackson, for being my kids.

And thank you, Erika, for being my wife. I adore you.